Swimming
in the
Deep End

Four Foundational Skills
for Leading Successful
School Initiatives

Jennifer Abrams
Foreword by Ellie Drago-Severson

Solution Tree | Press

a division of
Solution Tree

555 North Morton Street
Bloomington, IN 47404
800.733.6786 (toll free) / 812.336.7700
FAX: 812.336.7790

email: info@SolutionTree.com
SolutionTree.com

Visit **go.SolutionTree.com/leadership** to download the free reproducibles in this book.

Printed in the United States of America

Library of Congress Cataloging-in-Publication Data

Names: Abrams, Jennifer, author.
Title: Swimming in the deep end : four foundational skills for leading
    successful school initiatives / Jennifer Abrams.
Description: Bloomington, IN : Solution Tree Press, [2018] | Includes
    bibliographical references and index.
Identifiers: LCCN 2018045175 | ISBN 9781947604018 (perfect bound)
Subjects: LCSH: Educational leadership--United States. | Education--Aims and
    objectives--United States.
Classification: LCC LB2805 .A35 2018 | DDC 371.2--dc23 LC record available at https://lccn.loc.
gov/2018045175

Solution Tree
Jeffrey C. Jones, CEO
Edmund M. Ackerman, President

Solution Tree Press
President and Publisher: Douglas M. Rife
Associate Publisher: Sarah Payne-Mills
Art Director: Rian Anderson
Managing Production Editor: Kendra Slayton
Senior Production Editor: Tara Perkins
Senior Editor: Amy Rubenstein
Copy Editor: Miranda Addonizio
Proofreader: Kate St. Ives
Text and Cover Designer: Abigail Bowen
Editorial Assistant: Sarah Ludwig

Dedicated to my late father, Richard B. Abrams, who taught me how to truly swim at the age of three and supported me in whatever "deep end" I wanted to swim every year after.

—Jennifer

Acknowledgments

Much appreciation goes to the following people who sensed the need for discussion around this topic and who have supported me in ways they might never truly know. I am grateful.

To John Hebert, John Fredrich, Becki Cohn-Vargas, Danny Bauer, Elena Aguilar, Sharon Ofek, Ann Lorey, Ann Idzik, Claudia Frandsen, Sean O'Maonaigh, Dana Carmichael, Rod Berger, Ross Romano, Laura Marcus-Bricca, Barbara McAfee, Shivani Pulimamimidi, Meme Ratliff, and others who sat with me, fed me, and were willing to engage in discussion with me around this deep-end work.

To those in other school boards and school districts and educational organizations who added to and pushed the work forward: Heather Lageman and Liz Berquist at Baltimore County Public Schools, Region 13 Educational Service Center in Austin, Texas, the School of Education at William and Mary, Holly Couturier and Dick Durost at the Maine Principals Association, Jennifer Hicks, Kim Lilienthal and the Placer County Office of Education, and to those at Learning Forward and their affiliates who gave me space to shape this work, and to the participants at their conferences who encouraged me, participated in the workshops, and pushed my thinking.

To my behind-the-scenes supporters: my family who were my cheerleaders and guides—my late father, Richard Abrams; my late mother, Myrna Abrams; my brother and sister-in-law, Adam and Shelley Abrams; and my awesome nephews, Joe and Evan; who think I don't really work but just "fly around and talk to people."

To Solution Tree for being so supportive through the moments I couldn't work on the book but went into the deep-end end-of-life journey with the illness and eventual death of my father. To Douglas Rife, Claudia Wheatley, and Amy Rubenstein, thank you for your graciousness. The book is a better one thanks to your support.

Solution Tree Press would like to thank the following reviewers:

Jennette Barker
Principal
Henderson Elementary School
Saint Charles, Missouri

Michelle Davis
Instructional Literacy Coach
Gamble Rogers Middle School
Saint Augustine, Florida

Angy Dickson
Assistant Principal
Bryan Middle School
Saint Charles, Missouri

Andrew Grider
Principal
Rodney E. Thompson Middle School
Stafford, Virginia

Robert Johnson
Principal
Evergreen Middle School
Redmond, Washington

Paige Sanders
Principal
Henry A. Coffeen Elementary
Sheridan, Wyoming

Joy Wright
Principal
King Philip Middle School
West Hartford, Connecticut

Lisa Wunn
Principal
West Delaware Middle School
Manchester, Iowa

Table of Contents

About the Author

Jennifer Abrams is an international educational and communications consultant for public and independent schools, hospitals, universities, and nonprofits. In her twenty-six-year tenure at Palo Alto Unified School District in California, Jennifer led professional development sessions on topics from equity and elements of effective instruction to teacher leadership and peer coaching, and she facilitated teacher and administrator workshops at both the elementary and secondary levels. From 2000–2011, Jennifer was lead coach for the Palo Alto-Mountain View-Los Altos-Saratoga-Los Gatos Consortium's Beginning Teacher Support and Assessment Program. Jennifer trains and coaches teachers, administrators, nurses, hospital personnel, and others on new employee support, supervision, being generationally savvy, having hard conversations, and collaboration skills.

In her educational consulting work, Jennifer has presented at annual conferences such as Learning Forward, Association for Supervision and Curriculum Development (ASCD), National Association of Secondary School Principals, National Association of Elementary School Principals, and the New Teacher Center Annual Symposium, as well as at the Teachers' and Principals' Centers' Summer Institutes for International School Leadership. *Education Week*'s blog *Finding Common Ground* recognized Jennifer as one of twenty-one women all K–12 educators need to know, and the International Academy of Educational Entrepreneurship named her Entrepreneur of the Year. She has also been a featured interviewee on the topic of professionalism for ASCD's video series *Master Class*, hosted by National Public Radio's Claudio Sanchez.

Jennifer's publications include *Having Hard Conversations*, *The Multigenerational Workplace: Communicating, Collaborating and Creating Community*, and *Hard Conversations Unpacked—the Whos, the Whens and the What Ifs*. Jennifer writes a monthly newsletter blog, *Voice Lessons*, available on her website, www.jenniferabrams .com, and is a featured columnist for www.eSchoolnews.org writing about personal development for leaders.

Jennifer holds a bachelor's degree in English from Tufts University and a master's degree in education from Stanford University. To learn more about Jennifer's work, visit www.jenniferabrams.com or follow @jenniferabrams on Twitter.

To book Jennifer Abrams for professional development, contact pd@SolutionTree.com.

Foreword

By Ellie Drago-Severson

Jennifer Abrams has given us another gift—*Swimming in the Deep End: Four Foundational Skills for Leading Successful School Initiatives*. It is, for sure, a gift of love, born from her rich and deep experiences as a coach, international consultant, teacher, leader, and friend, working with leaders in schools, educational systems, health care, and various nonprofits around the globe. Throughout the book, Abrams encourages us to *swim in the deep end* by engaging with questions, using protocols, and employing practices she has designed thoughtfully and with dedicated intention. Each step of the way, she offers guidance—a roadmap—for how we can work individually and collectively toward making change by addressing *and living* the questions, and by learning more about ourselves and each other. Like most endeavors of great value, leading successful initiatives takes time, she explains. It takes hope. It takes trust. It takes patience. It takes care. It takes love. It takes dedication and commitment. It takes all of us. It is this kind of bringing together that Abrams seeks to support and achieve in this important work.

Specifically, *Swimming in the Deep End* focuses on knowing and understanding the challenges inherent in different initiatives so that our initiatives can make a difference. It also focuses on the importance of knowing one's own and others' values and paying attention to what schools and districts value as we implement important initiatives to bring about change and betterment. Throughout the book, Abrams offers many different kinds of learning lenses to help us understand these challenges and ourselves, so that we can more comfortably and confidently swim in the deep end as individuals and as a profession. The deep end, she wisely asserts, offers opportunities for us to grow and to help each other grow.

Not only does Abrams invite us to swim in the deep end and highlight the value of doing so, but she also shares courageously and powerfully some of the kinds of experiences we might consider—she calls these deep-end opportunities—that help us challenge and stretch ourselves and do the same for those in our care. Throughout her book, Abrams integrates and weaves together a tapestry of guiding questions, practices, and reflective questions that can help us to engage in four qualitatively different yet intimately connected *foundational deep end skills* that are linked to specific and vital internal capacities for leading successful school and system initiatives:

1. Thinking before we speak
2. Preempting resistance
3. Responding to resistance (for when we do speak)
4. Managing ourselves through change and resistance (after we speak) (p. 8)

Early on and throughout the book, Abrams reminds us that these are not only skills a person needs in and for the deep end, but also skills that will help each of us grow into fuller, more complete, and more effective versions of ourselves as leaders. This kind of stretching takes courage, Abrams notes, and her background as coach extraordinaire shines through especially clearly in the ideas, questions, and practices she offers to scaffold and support courageous change.

For example, as I read and reflected on the powerful chapters in Abrams's book, I was—and continue to be—reminded of Rainer Maria Rilke's (1993) thinking about questions:

> Be patient toward all that is unsolved in your heart and try to love the questions themselves, like locked rooms and like books that are now written in a very foreign tongue. Do not now seek the answers, which cannot be given you because you would not be able to live them. And the point is, to live everything. Live the questions now. Perhaps you will then gradually, without noticing it, live along some distant day into the answer. (p. 34)

Managing this—learning to live the questions—requires the internal capacity to manage complexity and ambiguity. Abrams's book helps us grow ourselves and in so doing it will help us support growth of others as well.

Abrams also reminds us of the critical significance of strong emotional, academic, and instructional supports—and how all of these are necessary for students and adults to lead and grow in schools and systems. Toward these ends, Abrams powerfully highlights that we don't have to swim in the deep end alone. We need each other. We need each other to trust and be trusting. We need each other to build trust where trust has been broken. We need each other to become better communicators. We need each other to see deeper into ourselves and each other. Like mirrors or windows that reflect back new possibilities, trusted coaches, guides, and resources like this book can remind us of the power we have to transform ourselves and our systems, as well as the beauty and importance of pausing—whether it's pausing to care for ourselves, care for others, smile, laugh, seek input, reflect on next steps, restore, or notice life every day.

For these reasons and more, Abrams's words will reach right inside your heart, mind, and soul: "I want my colleagues, worldwide, to *thrive*," she writes—on the first page of the book's introduction (p. 1). This hope, motivation, and intention lives throughout the pages of this book. She shows us how to build a better world together with hope and love. And, like change, this is a book that requires time and considered reflection. I encourage you, with all my heart, to invest your time and care into learning from Abrams and her wisdom. It will be a cherished gift you give yourself.

Introduction

I am interested in people who swim in the deep end.
    —Amy Poehler

When I turned forty-eight, I began feeling *older*. Like I wanted to take everyone's face into my hands and kiss his or her cheeks. Like I wanted to come over to the tables of participants at my workshops, lean over, and hug all of those who were doing the good day-to-day work in their schools. I was becoming maternal. Maybe not maternal; maybe more like a big sister. Everyone's protective big sister. After twenty-eight years in education, I was older than many who attended my workshops. I talked to my friend Barbara about my protective feelings, and she smiled with understanding and told me I was "eldering." Not becoming an elder per se, but *eldering*. I was and am, thank goodness, not just getting older but, I believe, also getting wiser. I am growing out of the ego-driven state of mind of my thirties and forties, and I have more firmly embraced the big-sister role. I want my colleagues, worldwide, to *thrive*. I want my fellow educators to proudly and effectively meet the challenges that education serves up to them each and every day. And, along with being the protective big sister, I am becoming a bit of the nagging and nudgy big sister as well. I want more *for* my colleagues and *from* my colleagues. I want us all to be able to swim in the deep end of the pool and to be around others who do the same.

The Deep End

What do I mean by swimming in the deep end? Well, at a young age, I attended swimming lessons at the nearby Howard Johnson hotel. At the beginning, we students sat at the edge of the pool. Then after a bit, we sat on the steps of the pool with our tushies and legs in the water, and we bent down to put our chins in the water and we blew bubbles. Then, in the next lesson we walked in up to our knees. Then stood in the shallow end with the water all the way up to our necks. Then our heads went below water! Soon we were treading water. Step by step, we were learning to swim but were *always* able to touch the bottom.

The day I remember vividly was when our swimming teacher Mr. Patton said it was time to swim under water all the way to the other side. *To the deep end.* I remember being incredibly nervous, but when I did it, I was thrilled. I had pushed myself. I found the strength and the ability and the discipline to hold my breath, pump my arms and legs and swim to the deep end. Fifty or so years later, and with decades of new teacher coaching under my belt, I have been there "blowing bubbles" with new teachers as they developed and honed their skills in the classroom. I have also worked with more experienced teachers as they pushed themselves in their careers, creating portfolios of their work and obtaining advanced credentials. I have coached teachers and administrators from their shallow ends to their deep ends, whatever that means to them. Teaching their own classes or leading schools are some of the ways educators swim without the safety net of being able to touch the bottom, but getting there sometimes requires guidance. As a coach and consultant, I have always tried to be like Mr. Patton, a guide on the side. It has been an honor.

Now, with the increased challenges that we face in education (see figure I.1 for an extensive list compiled from the Principal Life [n.d.] Facebook group) and a shortage of teachers and administrators, the field cannot afford to stay in the shallow end by continuing such practices as using sit and get instructional strategies or grouping students in the same ways we have for decades, to name just a few. From literacy strategies to whole-school change; from collaboration to equity and achievement for all; we need to swim in the deep end as a profession. We need to be able to work with all students so they grow socially, emotionally, and academically. We need the ability to work together collectively in teams. We need the discipline and the strength to sustain ourselves and our students through major curricular change and the development of additional student support programs, through working with new technologies and managing schools in times of increased bullying and worsening violence. We need to know how to swim in the deep end more than ever. We shortchange students when we do not address the increasingly complex challenges our students face. We must prepare our students for a world that requires them to have different skillsets than in the past: to be able to communicate globally, understand themselves intimately, be tech savvy and media literate, and so on. If we want to do what is right for our students we must up our game and venture into the deep end.

- Achieving academic and digital literacy for all
- Teaching digital citizenship
- Creating social-emotional learning programs
- Increasing academic achievement of students of color
- Emphasizing STEM
- Preparing and supporting teachers through mentoring, new teacher support, recruitment and retention practices, and intern programs
- Implementing changes to evaluation, assessment, and performance appraisal processes
- Engaging in leadership succession planning
- Ensuring student well-being and safety
- Eliminating inappropriate use of technology
- Addressing community and parental lack of understanding about students with special needs
- Addressing social media community pages where parents, students, and siblings are unkind in their comments about schools and school personnel
- Addressing mental health impacts on students, staff, school, families, and the community (depression, cutting, alcohol and drug use, mental health hospitalization, sexual orientation issues leading to suicide threats, and other challenges by those struggling with or affected by trauma)
- Improving deeply engrained negative school climates and cultures
- Creating new schooling paradigms through such practices as personalized learning, project-based learning, blended learning, and standards-based assessments
- Cultivating and maintaining an environment where the self-expectation of every teacher is to continue to grow professionally
- Responding to severe student behavior challenges through classroom management training and discipline practices that work
- Addressing standardized testing
- Diagnosing the causes of deep-seated lack of motivation and engagement
- Transforming teacher teams that are inflexible and resistant to change
- Ensuring supervision and evaluation that is productive and supports professional growth

Source: Adapted from Principal Life, n.d.

Figure I.1: Deep-end challenges in schools.

Deep-End Opportunities

If we are asking our colleagues to up their game and stretch themselves, then we also need to get into the deep end more often. One simple way I keep pushing myself to the deep end, at least in my mind, is by subscribing to blogs by people who inspire, but also slightly scare me. These writers are bruised by life but also emboldened and confident. They have successfully taken on a deep-end challenge or other difficult experience and gone on to support others who want to swim in the deep end too. They write, speak, facilitate, and create communities of like-minded folks. When I get invitations to join them in their deep ends, sometimes the time or monetary commitment required prohibits me from doing so, but honestly, in most cases, I am just too scared. I don't yet have the emotional bandwidth to swim with these folks. *Yet* is the operative word here.

Here are a few of the experiences for which I have *yet* to jump into the deep end and join.

- **altMBA (https://altmba.com):** Bestselling author Seth Godin (*Tribes, Purple Cow, What to Do When It's Your Turn*) facilitates an intense four-week online leadership and management workshop with participants from around the world all learning about how to create businesses that have a global impact.

- **Open Master's Alt*Div (www.openmasters.org/altdiv):** In this self-directed learning program, each member designs his or her own learning journey for the year. The members of this program, who might have thought about going to divinity school or into counseling, work in community with other Alt*Div students to create a product or a program to support the spiritual and emotional growth of the globe.

- **Warriors of the Spirit (http://margaretwheatley.com):** Margaret J. Wheatley, of *Leadership and the New Science* fame in the 1990s, offers a year-long training experience to strengthen participants' ability to be in "dedicated service to the human spirit."

Alas, the "shoulda couldas" don't help. The good news is that deep-end opportunities show up daily, if we want to accept them. In your work, they are going to show up every day as well.

Looking back, I did participate in events that took me to what was then my deep end of the pool. I joined in a year-long set of Courage to Teach retreats, which are based on Parker J. Palmer's (1998) book *The Courage to Teach: Exploring the Inner Landscape of a Teacher's Life* (www.couragerenewal.org). We explored the heart of a teacher through personal stories, reflections on classroom practice, and insights from poets and storytellers. I remember the afternoons in which we were to be in solitude. As an extrovert, asked to not interact with anyone but myself, those three-hour containers of silent time used to challenge me. Now I cherish my silence. Deep ends are different for each of us and change for us as we grow and develop.

One of my best deep-end experiences was at one of my favorite places in the world, Esalen Institute, a retreat center and learning environment on the Pacific coast in Big Sur, California, that, according to its website, is "devoted to cultivating deep change in self and society" (see www.esalen.org). I once spent a weekend there at a workshop led by teacher Sam Keen (2016), one of my cognitive crushes. In this workshop called *What's Next? Reviewing and Revisioning Our Lives*, those in attendance considered the following questions (see https://bit.ly/2QfdWEB).

- Where are you on your journey?
- What have you accomplished?
- What hasn't happened yet?
- What do you need to leave behind?
- For what, or for whom, are you grateful?
- What will your legacy will be?
- How will you fulfill the gift of your life?
- What decisions do you want to make?

I was afraid *for three years* of attending this workshop. Would I have to leave someone behind? What would I have to do next that freaked me out? I ultimately did leave a school district, and a beau, behind. And I am still standing. Deep end, what's next?

There are many books we can turn to that will help us with the deep ends in our personal lives. The self-help corner of the local bookstore is full of them. This particular book is about the *professional* deep-end work we do in schools: the projects we undertake, the initiatives we are tasked to move forward with, the teams we are in charge of. What I hope this book will do is support you in seeing what the deep-end skills, capacities, and mindsets look like for you in your context, with your work as an ever-learning education leader—someone who is growing his or her leadership skills to be effective within your school or organization, no matter your role. If you are looking for some strategies to stay afloat in the deep end, dive on in.

The Four Foundational Deep-End Skills

The Institute for Education Leadership (2013) in Ontario, Canada, outlines specific personal leadership resources undergirding a set of education leadership capacities for administrators in their province, as follows.

- Cognitive resources
  - Problem-solving expertise
    - Understanding and interpreting problems
    - Identifying goals
    - Articulating principles and values
    - Identifying constraints
    - Developing solution processes
    - Maintaining calm and confidence in the face of challenging problems
  - Knowledge about school and classroom conditions with direct effects on student learning
    - Technical or rational conditions
    - Emotional conditions
    - Organizational conditions
    - Family conditions
  - Systems thinking
    - Being able to understand the dense, complex, and reciprocal connections among different elements of the organization
    - Having foresight to engage the organization in likely futures and consequences for action
- Social resources
  - The ability to perceive emotions
    - Recognizing our own emotional responses
    - Discerning emotional responses in others through verbal and nonverbal cues
  - The ability to manage emotions
    - Reflecting on our own emotional responses and their potential consequences
    - Persuading others to likewise reflect on their responses
  - The ability to act in emotionally appropriate ways

- Being able to exercise control over which emotions guide our actions
- Being able to help others act on emotions that serve their best interests
- Psychological resources
  - Optimism
    - Habitually expecting positive results from our efforts
    - Recognizing where we have, and do not have, opportunities for direct influence and control
    - Taking positive risks
  - Self-efficacy
    - Believing in our own abilities to perform a task or achieve a goal
    - As a result of positive self-efficacy, taking responsible risks, expending substantial effort, and persisting in the face of initial failure
  - Resilience
    - Being able to recover from, or adjust easily to, change or misfortune
    - Being able to thrive in challenging circumstances
  - Proactivity
    - Being able to stimulate and effectively manage change on a large scale under complex circumstances
    - Showing initiative and perseverance in bringing about meaningful change

Their list is broad and applicable in many contexts. The Institute for Education Leadership (2013) writes:

> In addition to recognizing and undertaking effective leadership practices, effective leaders also tend to possess and draw on a small but critical number of personal leadership resources when enacting the leadership practices. There is a compelling research base for including cognitive, social and psychological resources. (p. 22)

Aspiring and emerging leaders should take note of these skills and mindsets and learn to develop them from the get-go; for more experienced leaders, the list is a terrific self-assessment for our continuing growth. The development of these three main capacities of personal leadership—the need for the development of (1) cognitive, (2) social, and (3) psychological resources—undergirds this book.

This book will look at the big-picture cognitive, social, and psychological capacities through a smaller frame and focus on the four foundational skills for leaders working in the deep end. The four foundational skills are as follows.

1. Thinking before we speak

2. Preempting resistance

3. Responding to resistance (for when we do speak)

4. Managing ourselves through change and resistance (after we speak)

These are not the *only* skills you need to swim in the deep end, but these skills will help you be more successful as you consider a new project or initiative that pushes you to uncharted waters in your leadership work. Those who are leading projects and initiatives for the first time as well as those who are more experienced but want to up their game for the next challenge that comes their way will benefit from cultivating these skills. Given that resistance to change is commonplace and inevitable, the focus on resistance in these foundational skills should not be unexpected. It is pervasive and normal. The skill sets we are building around anticipating resistance and verbally managing it when you encounter it will take a major role in this text. How to build up your ability to understand where it comes from and how to respond to it is key for leaders to effectively swim in the deep end.

The questionnaire in figure I.2 (pages 9–11) contains questions to guide you as you read the text in relation to your work at your school, and to help you see where you are in terms of the four foundational skills for deep-enders. The book is best read with a personal foundational case study in mind. Think of a real project or initiative you are beginning or will begin soon. (For examples of initiatives, see the list of deep-end challenges in schools [figure I.1, page 3].) The deep-end self-assessment questions provide the basis for the contents of the rest of the book. It is important to complete this assessment before moving on to the subsequent chapters, and to have it readily available as you work through chapters 1 through 4. This assessment, like all preassessments, is central to scaffolding the learning to come. Taking a minute to consider the questions as you begin gives you a sense of the whole and connects your work to this book so the text can be more relevant and timely for you in your work. Completing this assessment will also help you determine which chapters of the book you might want to focus on more deeply as you increase your capacity to be even more effective as a leader in your school. Responding to these questions will help you identify where you might have *learning edges*—areas where you need to grow and improve. Use the + or – column in figure I.2 to annotate where you might feel you need some more support for your project or initiative as you move forward. Mark a + for items that are strengths and a – for items you need to work on. I will address each of these questions as the book progresses.

Thinking Before You Speak	+ or –
1. Do I know what challenge or challenges this initiative is solving?	
2. Do I know whether this challenge requires solving a problem or reaching a compromise? Can I speak to this difference?	
3. Do I know what I value and how this project aligns with the values I hold?	
4. Do I know what values my school or district emphasizes, and can I communicate how this initiative aligns with those values?	
5. Have I thought through who needs to be involved in the planning of this initiative?	
6. Do I know how to get others' input in a way that is useful for me and that they see as worthwhile?	
7. Do I have good facilitation skills and know how to lead groups through project design and implementation?	
8. If I have decision-making authority, do I communicate processes and decisions with transparency to all stakeholders?	
9. Can I tell a story or narrative about this challenge and decision so others will feel the need for this initiative to move forward?	
10. Can I share data, evidence, or research about this challenge and decision so others will understand the need for this initiative to move forward?	
11. Do I know and can I communicate what my action plan is for implementation?	
12. Now that I have an action plan in place, do I know how I will communicate this message?	
13. Am I aware that there may be covert processes at work that I might not be able to address?	
14. Have I intentionally designed stop-and-reflect moments into the process of implementation?	

Figure I.2: Deep-end self-assessment—four foundational skills.

continued ►

Preempting Resistance	+ or −
1. Do I know what questions and concerns most commonly come up with a new initiative and how I might address them early in the rollout process?	
2. Do I know the people I am working with in some personal way (for example, their ages, family status, ethnicity, and so on)?	
3. Am I aware of adult learning theory and how it might connect to the initiative I am implementing?	
4. Do I understand the psychological threat-or-reward instinct so I can mitigate fears during my communications?	
5. Am I mindful that others are at different developmental stages in their own growth and that I need to communicate with them differently? How might this initiative challenge them, and how might I support them to move forward with the initiative?	

Responding to Resistance	+ or −
1. Given that resistance will happen, do I know ways I can professionally respond to those who will respond negatively to the initiative?	
2. Do I have an awareness of how my body language is perceived so I am viewed as credible or approachable, as the situation requires?	

Managing Oneself Through Change and Resistance	+ or −
1. Do I have structures and supports in place in my life (for example, exercise, healthy eating, massage, and sleep) to help me physically manage the challenges that will come my way?	
2. Do I have a breathing, meditation or quieting practice that will help bring calm to my body and mind?	
3. Do I take time to cultivate relationships in my life outside work (for example, with family, friends, a partner, or pets)?	
4. Do I have a structure in my life for acknowledging the good that is going on or a method of expressing gratitude on a continual basis?	
5. Am I aware of the concept of a growth versus fixed mindset, and how am I working with it in my own life and work?	
6. Do I have self-talk that is optimistic, and am I learning to be more optimistic? (Do I have a coach or someone who works with me on my self-talk and helps me look at my assumptions, belief systems, and strengths?)	

7. Do I have a compassion practice that includes both self-compassion and loving kindness for others?	
8. Do I take time out for inspirational moments that bring me back to why I do what I do for students and ground me in the importance of doing deep-end work (for example, TED Talks, spiritual centers, churches, synagogues, retreat centers, readings, author talks, or podcasts)?	
9. Do I have plans to grow myself and my skill sets (for example, through conferences, mentoring groups, online courses, professional learning communities, or reading lists)?	
10. Do I take time for restorative moments?	
11. Do I notice that I laugh every day? Do I put myself in situations that make me smile?	
12. Do I have moments when I can experience giving in a different way outside my work, perform acts of service, or attend events that support causes?	

Visit **go.SolutionTree.com/leadership** *for a reproducible version of this figure.*

School-improvement initiatives, with their never-ending challenges, provide us with amazing opportunities to swim in the deep end. They require us to have robust cognitive skills, social acumen, linguistic facility, and psychological strength. This book is an attempt to give you some resources and strategies to strengthen your ability, no matter your role, to swim more confidently in the deep end. While I cannot be there to lift you back into the boat when your mask fills with water, I will try my best to help you have strategies to tread water and stay afloat.

About This Book

When I share the swimming in the deep end metaphor with others for the first time, it brings forth many reactions. I tell folks I want to write for readers who want to push themselves to be more capable and courageous during moments of change. Some of the responses I receive include the following.

- "Hmm . . ."

- "You know, some might really want to be in the shallow end. That's deep enough for them."

- "You might lose a lot of readers if you go too far ahead of them."

- "Some folks don't want to know how to swim in the deep end. They are exhausted. Can the book just be a life jacket? Or a boat to come rescue them?"

I understand the concerns. Leaders have had little time to learn how to swim in the deep end and have either thrown themselves in for the sake of the students or have been put in deep waters without the supports they need. Leaders are struggling to breathe before they even really begin an initiative, and they burn out fast. Mental health challenges and turnover of administrators is seen in schools daily, and both the schools and the students suffer.

While this book isn't an immediate Coast Guard rescue, it does provide support from the perspective of a swimming teacher—a Mr. Patton if you will—to help you *build* the skills to swim in the deep end and support you in facing whatever change is coming to you or that you are making happen at your site. We need to build up our strength cognitively, socially and psychologically so we can be more self-sufficient and swim in the deep end for longer. Our students need us.

Who This Book Is For

This book is not for everyone. This book isn't for those who do not want to progress beyond blowing bubbles. It will challenge you. Yet it is meant to empower you. It is for those who want to build skills that will help move schools and the profession forward. It is for those who want to have more impact, no matter their role. It is for those who have been assigned an initiative to implement and are in need of some guidance and support to be successful. We all have roles in which we discover our credential programs did not teach us what it takes to do the work, and in which we need more cognitive, social, and psychological skills to be effective. These are what I refer to as *deep-end skills*.

If any of the following statements resonate with you, or you are an aspiring leader with no definitive leadership task ahead of you, yet you want to be even more prepared when you get a leadership role, this is your book.

- "I have this job, and I want to be successful, but I have no idea how to roll out this initiative I was just tasked to make happen."
- "I was just told I am the person in charge of this project for the upcoming school year. What now?"
- "I have an idea I really would like to move forward in my school but there is so much pushback every time I bring it up."

- "I know we have a lot on our plates but we still need to move ahead with a new curriculum because it is best for students. How do I negotiate the balance of caring for the teachers but dealing with the urgency of student needs?"

- "I became a leader because I see things can be better, and I want to make them better. And yet every day is a challenge, and I am overwhelmed. What do I need to know to stay afloat?"

You may be thinking, "What if I am an experienced leader who has rolled out quite a few initiatives? Can I still benefit from reading this book?" While some who pick up this book may be new to leadership or administrative roles, experienced leaders can also benefit from the ideas in this book. Some of the benefits it provides experienced leaders include, but are not limited to:

- Affirmation and validation of your existing work and efforts (and that is a good reason to read a book—to know you know a few things! How wonderful is that?)

- Reminders of a few things you want to be more consistent at doing in your role as a leader

- New strategies as you move along on your leadership journey

- Guidelines and support for your work as a mentor or coach of aspiring and emerging leaders

This book is a primer. A beginning. It doesn't address in depth *every* skill you need to roll out a new idea, project, or initiative, or to take the lead in a group or a program, or to become a master administrator, but it is a good start. To paraphrase Abraham Maslow (as cited in Tracy, 2010), one will either step forward into growth or step backward into safety. This book will help you step *forward*.

How This Book Is Organized

As mentioned previously, there are certain cognitive, social, and psychological skills necessary for swimming in the deep end. I have identified four foundational skills for deep-end leadership: (1) thinking before you speak, (2) preempting resistance, (3) responding to resistance, and (4) managing yourself through change and resistance. These skills provide the main structure for this book no matter what your deep-end challenge will be; change management and resistance-related skills in this book cross all initiatives. From blended learning to changes in the mathematics curriculum at a school, from focusing more on wellness to moving from Advanced Placement to

International Baccalaureate programs, change is change, and change often begets resistance. The concept of resistance and being aware of it, no matter the challenge, is a foundational skill.

Chapter 1 starts with the first of the four foundational skills for deep-end leadership: thinking before you speak. This chapter focuses on planning before beginning an initiative. If you have tasks and projects under your purview or you are asked to move a specific initiative forward, thinking before you speak and take action is critical. What do you need to think through before you roll out an initiative? What questions can you anticipate others will have for you as you begin a project or introduce a new program? How can you align this work with something that the folks at your site already value and support? How can you make sense of something in terms of both its story and the data so you connect with different types of colleagues as the rollout begins? How will you communicate a coherent plan while still knowing there are so many bumps in the road that you won't anticipate?

Chapter 2 discusses the second foundational skill: preempting resistance. This chapter focuses on the ever-present need for understanding others that will arise when leaders present something new. Since pushback is a given when a leader brings forth an initiative, what might we need to know in order to work even more effectively with others at this crucial juncture? We examine filters of perception and how seeing through your colleagues' eyes might assist you in preempting resistance, as well as learning about the neurology of threat so others can work with you in a more safe, understandable way.

Chapter 3 explores our third skill: how to respond to resistance once it occurs. This is social awareness *in action*. How do we speak to one another, promote a given point of view constructively, and articulate our perspectives with strength but without rigidity? What nonverbal and verbal skills do we need? How can we advocate effectively in both verbal and nonverbal ways?

Chapter 4 addresses the fourth foundational skill for deep-end work: managing yourself through change and resistance. Do you have structures and supports in place in your life to help you physically manage the challenges and challenging moments that will come your way? How do you stay calm in the face of conflict? How do you manage stress over the long term? This chapter shares strategies and techniques for managing *yourself* as you swim in the deep end.

Each of these four chapters dives into key questions I believe leaders need to be especially mindful of if they want to swim in the deep end. I explain each of these questions and offer resources or strategies to use in order to answer these questions more effectively as the chapter moves forward. After each question, I provide additional information or suggest resources that will help you stretch to make sure you have answered the question to the degree necessary to move forward with confidence.

The epilogue concludes our work in this book by answering the question, What is next? As this book is meant to establish the *beginning* of deep-end work, and is not the final word, you must ask yourself where you need to move to next on your leadership journey. This epilogue gives you some ideas of where you *might* want to go in the deep end of learning.

I offer reflection questions at the end of each chapter for individual readers, professional learning group discussions, or book studies to prompt readers to bring what they have learned from the book into the real world. These questions will involve you in conversation so you can evolve and then apply the work to your setting and context.

I have also included appendices with additional content to support your deep-end work. Appendix A includes links to online resources for building resilience. Appendix B lists online resources you can access to help you dive deeper into the concepts you encounter in this book. Visit **go.SolutionTree.com/leadership** for free reproducible versions of these appendices. Additionally, visit www.jenniferabrams.com/inspiration for a collection of inspirational quotes to keep yourself and your colleagues inspired to do deep-end work.

Now, on to the deep end. A Buddhist scripture says, "Few are they among humans, / The people who reach the short beyond. / But these other folk / Only run along the [hither] bank" (Carter & Palihawadana, 2000, p. 17). In schools, given the urgency and the importance of our work, we cannot just run up and down on this side of the river. We need to do more. We need to cross over. To do that we need to head into the deep end. Let's jump in.

Reflection Questions

Wade into the following questions for team or individual reflection.

- What does swimming in the deep end mean for you?

- What deep-end challenges do you feel you are facing at this time?

- Before you read through the chapters that follow, what are you most intrigued by or think will be useful to you?

- What deep-end learning opportunities have you passed up? Which ones did you take advantage of?

- In what deep-end professional learning opportunities might you engage in the next few years?

- As you take the self-assessment with regard to a specific project or initiative at your site, where do you find yourself feeling validated? Where do you find some learning edges?

- As you reflect on items in your self-assessment that contain learning edges for you, which ones can you research online for more information, or which books can you begin reading to access some new strategies? To find books to access new strategies, a good starting place is the References and Resources section in this book (page 91).

CHAPTER 1

Thinking Before You Speak

Direction over speed.
—Shane Parrish

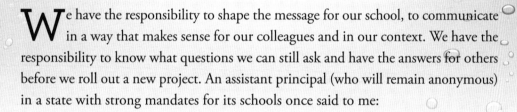

We have the responsibility to shape the message for our school, to communicate in a way that makes sense for our colleagues and in our context. We have the responsibility to know what questions we can still ask and have the answers for others before we roll out a new project. An assistant principal (who will remain anonymous) in a state with strong mandates for its schools once said to me:

> What do I need to know about thinking and planning before we speak? Everything is just given to us from above. We don't get to think. We are just the messengers. I have no control over what I implement. Just give me the answer to how to deal with the resistance that will come when I tell others what needs to change now.

I truly believe that however we feel about what is "given to us from above," we still have the responsibility to frame it for our coworkers who will be implementing it. While it is true that the country, state, province, district, or school administration (whoever is "above" you in the hierarchy) is telling you to make it work, you still have the responsibility to shape that message and own your part in the process. This requires emotional intelligence and cognitive ability.

In an article for *Psychology Today*, Adam Grant (2014a), professor at the Wharton School at University of Pennsylvania and author of *Give and Take*, cites a systematic review by researchers Dana Joseph and Dan Newman (2010) that examines comprehensive data from all extant studies at the time, testing the influence of emotional intelligence and cognitive ability on job performance. Grant (2014a) explains, "In

Joseph and Newman's comprehensive analysis, cognitive ability accounted for more than 14 percent of job performance. Emotional intelligence accounted for less than 1 percent."

Well, boo. Does this mean *our* study of emotional intelligence is worthless and we just need to get cognitively more capable? Luckily, no. Read on.

Grant (2014a) says:

> This isn't to say that emotional intelligence is useless. It's relevant to performance in jobs where you have to deal with emotions every day, like sales, real estate, and counseling. If you're selling a house or helping people cope with tragedies, it's very useful to know what they're feeling and respond appropriately. But in jobs that lack these emotional demands—like engineering, accounting, or science—emotional intelligence predicted lower performance. . . . If your job is to fix a car or balance numbers in a spreadsheet, paying attention to emotions might distract you from working efficiently and effectively.

Teaching does not lack emotional demands. Educators are in the people business, the development business, the teaching and learning business, which requires us to possess emotional intelligence. And honestly, while we need to be aware of the emotions of those with whom we work, there are also those moments when we need to focus on being practical, look at the facts and use our noggins to plot out a plan.

Deep-end abilities are varied and complex. Some are more cognitive, others more social, and still others psychological in nature. It isn't an either-or situation in the deep end. We need all of these skills, and in this chapter we focus on thinking before you speak and planning for when you do speak. First, we examine why planning is important for a new initiative, then we review each of the self-assessment questions for thinking before you speak, in detail, to help you gauge your strengths and weaknesses with each item.

The Importance of Planning

In classrooms, educators write lesson *plans*, instruct, and assess. In receiving feedback from students and learning what worked and didn't work, we rethink and we revise. Many times, we may find there were misconceptions we didn't plan to address because we didn't lesson plan well enough and confusion among our students because we didn't teach or scaffold certain concepts effectively. We know that when we don't plan, things don't go as smoothly as they could have.

The same happens on a larger scale with rollouts of initiatives in schools. For some reason, (maybe we weren't given enough time to plan, or we have pressure from above to get it done now, and so on) we hurry, we don't spend enough time thinking before we speak, and we roll things out in a sloppy way. It gets us in trouble, over and over and over. Aspiring and emerging leaders need to think before they speak. Direction before speed.

I can hear you already. *This rollout is urgent. Students need our support now, and this change has to happen this semester.* I understand these pressures, but to be clear, I am not suggesting we slow down to a snail's pace, create endless committees to provide input, or navel-gaze ad nauseam. However, we can consider some deep-end thinking skills to put to use throughout the thinking and planning process.

Teachers reflect on lessons, review data, consider next steps, and make decisions about those next steps. They then plan the next lesson, teach it, and gather more feedback. Considering these facts, cycles of planning and reflection are most likely not absolutely new to you and, while it is different in the sense that you are now working with adults around a school change initiative, you already know those fundamental steps, so breathe easier. You have seen this cycle of action before. The next section will provide processes and decision-making tools to assist with this deep-end challenge.

A Deep Dive Into Self-Assessment Questions

You should have already completed the deep-end self-assessment around your initiative or project in the introduction (see figure I.2, pages 9–11). In the remainder of this chapter, we reflect on questions from your deep-end self-assessment that focus on the first of the four foundational deep-end skills—thinking before you speak—and determine for which questions you have a learning edge.

Question 1: Do I Know What Challenge or Challenges This Initiative Is Solving?

Deep-end leaders work hard at articulating the real challenge they are trying to solve. It is important for leaders to closely examine what the challenge is and then determine if what they want to have happen is congruent to that objective. Will the challenge be adequately addressed if this initiative gets rolled out? Will this new center, curriculum, or teaching strategy move toward the goal to lessen or erase this challenge? There is a huge benefit to knowing your intent and then choosing a response that aligns well. The following co-teaching case study is but one rollout that didn't need to happen as it did—it could have been more successful if the challenge-framing process had been just a bit more rigorous.

Case Study in Challenge Framing:
The Co-Teaching Challenge

A student support director knew she believed in inclusion of students with special needs, and wanted to do more push-in support (support provided within the general education classroom) for students receiving additional assistance versus taking them out of class and placing them in resource classes. She had been at workshops and done some research on the effectiveness of co-teaching, and decided to roll out co-teaching in ninth-grade classrooms, pairing resource teachers with content-specific teachers for the following fall. She made the pairings and put a day of training on the books. The content-specific teachers thought of resource teachers as supports for specific students they had in their classrooms. The resource teachers self-identified as experts at understanding learning differences and being case workers for their students but did not consider being co-teachers as part of their professional identity—colleagues at the same school, maybe, but not co-educators in the same room.

Teachers attended a mandatory one-day training on what was expected as of the start of the school year. The training explained that now everyone would be working together (with expected parity) in the same room several hours a day. No common prep was factored in. The rollout began. It wasn't an immediate success, nor was it a complete success several years later. There were power struggles, hurt feelings, and a lot of confusion. The big question that teachers and parents continue to ask and should be asking is whether this program has been helpful for student growth and well-being. The conversation continues.

In this scenario, the student support director believed that students needed to be in general education classrooms for a longer portion of the day. She wanted to live out the idea of inclusion in practice to improve instruction for all, but she didn't take into deep consideration the dynamics on the ground for those who would implement it. If she had studied the challenge a bit more before making this decision, might the implementation have gone more smoothly? Most likely. In this scenario, the response seemed reactive and somewhat personal. The director cared deeply about making change to do more push-in instruction, but the teachers felt blindsided and insulted by it being sprung on them at the end of the year, as many needed to change their schedules and had little time for collaborating, communicating, and preparing to shift their practice. Being more proactive when implementing this change could have improved the outcome. For example, if you are encountering ideas at conferences that you think will make life better (such as new evaluation systems, different curricula, and so on) and you want to bring them into your school or district, are you sure that the solution you put into place will fix the problem you might have? Not only knowing what your challenge is but also knowing whether the initiative you are implementing is the right fix really is an essential deep-end skill.

You may be asking yourself, "But what if I don't get to decide what the challenge is and I am responsible for the rollout just the same?" If the state or the school's board of education has already determined without your input to implement a new initiative, you still have a responsibility to see where this diagnosis came from and to understand its origins. While it might be that no one asked for your input and now it is a problem and an emergency for you and your colleagues, it still is something to research, to understand, and to begin to frame a plan of implementation around. Why? Because your colleagues will look to you as the person to articulate where this challenge came from and how this initiative will be a part of the solution.

And while you can build up your sphere of influence so that next time the higher-ups roll something out they might ask for your input *ahead* of the changes, understanding the framing of *this* challenge will help shape the communication and implementation plan for this initiative going forward. You have the responsibility as a deep-end leader to know what challenge this initiative is solving and to communicate this thinking to your colleagues.

Question 2: Do I Know Whether This Challenge Requires Solving a Problem or Reaching a Compromise? Can I Speak to This Difference?

When deep-end leaders work to frame challenges, it is important to recognize you may not always be dealing with a problem that has a direct solution. Instead, the situation may present a polarity you must work to manage. Knowing the difference between a polarity and a problem will help you to better focus your efforts and shape your communications. Problems are solvable. For instance, finding a time when everyone can attend a meeting or determining what to add to the agenda for the parent meeting are problems with solutions. Polarities are to be *managed*. Polarities include things like achieving better balance between common aspects of our assessments and what is up to each individual teacher and dedicating more time to focusing on teacher well-being rather than focusing solely on student well-being; these are challenges to be managed.

Just as we need to both inhale and exhale and can't do one without the other, polarities are not an either-or situation but instead *yes and* kind of work. In education, we often hear of certain *pendulum swings*, from a focus on whole child or the focus on back-to-basics academics; from a focus on the art of teaching to the science of teaching. Swinging from one side to the other causes both sides to get defensive and protective, and no divergent and other-focused thinking can happen when a side is in fight or flight mode. No one can—as much as others might want them to—cowboy up (that is, intentionally determine to overcome a challenge) while in this frame of mind. Jane A. G. Kise's (2014) *Unleashing the Positive Power of Differences: Polarity Thinking in Our Schools* is an excellent book that "provides tools and processes for avoiding those pendulum swings by listening to the wisdom of multiple points of view" (p. 2). This involves a focus on both sides of a polarity.

For example, consider how a polarity was approached when one of the principals in a school district in which I worked rolled out common assessments as the next year's must-do. The principal told the teachers that things were changing and the district would dictate their common assessments. Teachers went crazy; they were accustomed to and still wanted autonomy in their classrooms and in their practice. If the administrator had instead communicated what teachers needed to align and what they could do with autonomy, rather than focusing just on the aligning assessment aspect of teacher practice, it might not have appeared that she was disrespecting teachers. The polarity discussion might have been more successful and resulted in greater buy-in from the teachers if she had framed the assessment shift as part of a polarity to support common achievement, and highlighted what *wasn't* going change (instructional strategies) alongside what *was* going to change (assessments).

On the other hand, consider the example of another school where tradition rules. There has always been a capstone project that is the cornerstone of what makes this school unique. So what happens if a new principal encourages the school to reconsider how that project can be designed? Does it stay as-is because "we have always done it that way"? Old ways aren't inherently wrong. New ways of looking at things aren't either. There *is* a middle ground, *and* it needs to be discussed and facilitated so both sides interpret taking on the challenge not as an either-or but rather a *yes and* moment. If the leader determines this presents a problem to be solved, his or her response would end up dismissing one side of the story. However, if the leader looks at it as managing a polarity, he or she can make improvements by considering other perspectives. If you frame the polarity as a problem, you run the risk of causing the initiative to fail before it's begun. The following list offers common polarities leaders may face in schools. Deep-end leaders see these topics as manageable polarities rather than problems in need of a prescribed solution.

- Autonomy and collaboration
- Team relationships and team tasks
- Clarity and flexibility
- Continuity and change
- Work priorities and home priorities
- Needs of students and needs of staff
- Teacher as lecturer and teacher as facilitator
- Centralization and decentralization
- School responsibility and social responsibility

Question 3: Do I Know What I Value and How This Project Aligns With the Values I Hold?

Before beginning to determine how to implement an initiative, it is essential for your credibility that you are able to articulate how the project aligns with your values. After all, beyond all the hype or the noise, the research and the recognition, one must know what one stands for. What are your beliefs? What values do you want to make sure undergird your work? It will feel inauthentic if you cannot state how this initiative aligns with your values. This is *not* to say you must ignore the school's values (see the next question beginning on page 24 for a discussion of engaging with the school). Yet, if you are attempting to support an initiative you can't buy into, others will know, and others will recognize your support for the initiative is not genuine.

Stan Slap (2010), author of *Bury My Heart at Conference Room B: The Unbeatable Impact of Truly Committed Managers* asks leaders in his company that they live their values inside and outside of the workplace—not just for the eight hours of work they do inside the building. He is interested in his colleagues being authentic and living out their beliefs 24/7 because it is painful to not believe in what you are doing. It hurts. It takes a physical and emotional toll. Susan Scott (2004) illustrates this idea by quoting her colleague Pat Murray, "If you want to see someone in real pain watch someone who knows who he is and defaults on it on a regular basis" (p. 62). What values do you want to live aloud in this deep-end project or initiative you are working on, and can you put those values front and center as you firmly set your compass? Consider how your values align with your school's values. As Peter Block (personal communication, 2013) says, "Do you walk bent over in compromise every day you go do your job or do you walk into work standing tall?" Wouldn't it be great to start out standing tall with the work you do?

Got Values, Anyone?

Knowing how you and your values align with the initiative is critical. For example, if you value compassion and the initiative is about social-emotional learning there is a good fit. Or if you value competence or achievement, then working on getting the advanced placement program to be something for more students might be a good fit. Look up a list of values—visit https://jamesclear.com/core-values to see one list. Can you see how your school's core values from this list align with the initiative you are implementing?

Now, review the mission and vision statements from your school and district. How can you communicate about this project using the language of the mission or vision statements? For example, if the mission statement includes "be resilient, responsible, respectful," does this initiative align well with those goals?

Consider the initiatives your school has implemented in the last two or three years. Ask those who lead them how the values of the school undergird those initiatives.

Question 4: Do I Know What Values My School or District Emphasizes, and Can I Communicate How This Initiative Aligns With Those Values?

Knowing the values your school or district stands for is another key prerequisite for implementing a successful deep-end initiative. Do you know what your school or district values? Perhaps a district wants students to be resilient, responsible, and respectful. Another's mission statement may say it is student centered, fearless, social-justice minded, and diversity driven. Consider how your initiative makes the values of your school or district come alive and live out those values. Being true to your own and your district's values can be a big help, if not essential, as you roll out an initiative. Your buy-in and alignment with district values are critical. As mentioned previously, inauthenticity is something your colleagues can sense. If you don't believe in the project, your disconnect with the project will come across immediately. You need to find the words to describe to people why you believe in the project *and* why those working on the project should too. This articulation of the alignment of the project with the school's mission and vision can ground the work in something bigger than the project itself and can be so helpful for you and for those who will be doing the work.

Think about the initiative you are using as a guide as you read this book and respond to and examine the questions in figure I.2 (pages 9–11). If the higher-ups didn't hand it to you to implement as soon as possible, and you have time to design it, seek input, and decide how to roll it out, read on to the discussions of questions 5 through 8 (pages 25–28) in this chapter. If this is not the case, and your initiative requires you to go straight to implementation without input, move on to question 9 (page 29). However, while questions 5 to 8 may not be applicable for you at this moment, the deep-end questions they pose are certainly good to consider for next time. Revisit those questions for a future initiative.

Question 5: Have I Thought Through Who Needs to Be Involved in the Planning of This Initiative?

Resistance to a new initiative takes many forms. One common response from resistors is, "Why wasn't I included in the planning of this rollout?" To avoid creating resistors based on this valid complaint, getting input is critical. While there comes a time when you cannot include everyone in an initiative's planning and rollout, including the right stakeholders in the planning in authentic ways is important. It is best to include in the conversation members of the given constituency whom the initiative will affect as early as possible. Leaders of a new initiative can involve these individuals in a number of ways, including conducting surveys and town hall meetings, having team leads gather input from department members, and working on committees with stakeholders. Does it take time? Yes. Asking the question, "Does anyone have anything to say? Okay, well, it's settled," to a group of one hundred constituents at 4:45 p.m. does *not* qualify as getting input from the whole staff. Project planning that involves many stakeholders in the conversation requires the ability to plan ahead as well as excellent facilitation skills. To implement preplanning, the following questions may be appropriate to consider: Do all teachers need to have input in the decision of how this initiative will move forward? Just some? Do you need to include other stakeholders? Parents, classified staff? Students?

Question 6: Do I Know How to Get Others' Input in a Way That Is Useful for Me and That They See as Worthwhile?

If you are looking to get input into the design of the program or the change you are going to undertake, it is critical that you explain what kind of input you are asking for. After all, someone has taken time out of her day to give you some input. She will want to know how you will use it. In facilitation, we call this the *sandbox discussion*. Those giving you input need to know what "sandbox" they are playing in so they understand their role.

Before you conduct a focus group, release a survey, meet with departments to get their take, or hold a team meeting, you need to know what the end goal is. Be able to answer the following questions.

- What challenge are we gathering input on?
- Which values that we want to live as a school undergird this conversation?
- What is the process we will use for input gathering?
- What is the time frame for gathering this input? (Is this the only opportunity to put in your two cents?)
- How will we use the input from this meeting?
- Along with this group, who else will be sharing ideas?

Being able to provide answers to these questions and clarify the structure around which everyone will be working helps you have productive sandbox discussions by ensuring those who are sharing with you understand how they fit into the planning of this initiative.

You'll also need to consider the best methods for gathering the input—surveys, focus groups, whole-staff meetings, small-team meetings, one-on-ones? What's doable? What is your time frame, and how can you gather the correct information given the parameters? In my work, I have seen some initiatives fall short of obtaining buy-in because leaders did not consider the best ways to provide staff with clarity on the scope of their role in the initiative in order to gather meaningful input. For example, a staff might see three PowerPoint slides and have ten minutes of discussion at a staff meeting, which half the staff doesn't attend, and during which the other half of the staff isn't ever sure how to share their input or if the decision was a *fait accompli* and already made. Be transparent and open as well as realistic about what kinds of input you will take into consideration and the roles of those who are sharing their ideas.

It is worth your time to invest in professional learning to strengthen the deep-end skill of facilitating discussion. The Thinking Collaborative (www.thinkingcollaborative .com) does great work on how to gather input, as does Elena Aguilar (2016) in her book *The Art of Coaching Teams*.

Question 7: Do I Have Good Facilitation Skills and Know How to Lead Groups Through Project Design and Implementation?

In the lesson plans teachers design, they devise activities that will engage students in work congruent to the learning. With a desire to get diverse opinions and to make sure all voices are heard in the design process, we, too, need processes to help think before we speak and plan our work with staff members. There are a variety of authors who write about facilitation skills and speak to the difference between dialogue and brainstorming as well as decision making and discussion. They supply protocols which, if leaders use them intentionally, can open up a great conversation that provides space for all to contribute and be heard. Refer to the feature box on this page for starting points on seeking out guidance on facilitation protocols.

A word of caution: many educators have told me that structures, protocols, norms, and time frames might constrict some folks and make them feel claustrophobic. They tell me some adults consider the structures patronizing and feel belittled, as those who use them are working under the assumption that without them the group wouldn't be able to have a discussion. To avoid this, when I work with educators, I share the purpose of the structure or protocol I am using and the value I hope everyone will get from using it, highlighting that it will ensure more participants get an opportunity to talk, that the group hears a multitude of perspectives, that the way we speak will be as humane as possible, or that the time frames will allow for the efficient use of time. Processes and facilitation allow us to focus more on the content and the work at hand.

Resources for Dialogue, Discussion, and Decision Making

- *The Adaptive School: A Sourcebook for Developing Collaborative Groups* (Garmston & Wellman, 1999)
- Liberating Structures (www.liberatingstructures.com)
- National School Reform Faculty (www.nsrfharmony.org)
- School Reform Initiative (www.schoolreforminitiative.org)
- *The Power of Protocols: An Educator's Guide to Better Practice* (McDonald, Mohr, Dichter, & McDonald, 2003)
- Thinking Collaborative (www.thinkingcollaborative.org)

Question 8: If I Have Decision-Making Authority, Do I Communicate Processes and Decisions With Transparency to All Stakeholders?

If you are gathering with a group to determine the end goal, how to move forward in addressing your challenge, or the implementation process you will use, and these decisions aren't simply handed to you from above, you are truly in the deep end. This requires group facilitation and decision-making skills, and the ability to design an implementation plan for working together to come up with the end goal. This is now a bigger process—facilitating a group discussion, dialogue, and eventual decisions can be as important as the ultimate decision itself. People won't just say, "What am I supposed to do now?" They will also ask, "Why wasn't I involved?" "When did this decision get made?" "Who gave input?" "How did this come to pass?" So a deep-end leader knows that both a transparent process and the transparency around the eventual product are both important communication pieces to the successful implementation of the initiative. Make the process as transparent as possible. To get started, consider who will and should be involved, over what period of time they will be involved, how much input and dialogue will occur before you make a decision, and how you will make the decision (for example, by consensus, vote, and so on). Ultimately, the transparency of the process will help you. I am not trying to be reductive or simplistic. This part of thinking before you speak might take *several* meetings and several months. Keep asserting and grounding the work in the mission, vision, and values of the school; continue to be clear about the challenge, transparent about the process of decision making, and cognizant of biases; and use communication structures to gather diverse points of view. Using norms so all group members' input is valued and all members feel safe sharing their points of view, having a clear understanding of the difference between how one might inquire and how one might advocate, and having a deep awareness of how decision making will take place for this group are all essential. Decision-making protocols and facilitation skills can be found at the websites mentioned in question 7 in this chapter (page 27). There will still be pushback from those who were not present or participating on the committee, and that's normal, but a clear understanding of how you or others made this decision will be invaluable to those who will do the work.

But just telling someone *what* the plan is with no sense of *why* or *how* will fall short. The next two questions speak to providing the *why* along with an action plan full of support, and the two questions after that will address the *how*.

Question 9: Can I Tell a Story or Narrative About This Challenge and Decision so Others Will Feel the Need for This Initiative to Move Forward?

As I mentioned in question 1, communication is necessary to ensure buy-in before you put the plan into place. One impactful communication method, storytelling, can cause a large part of our being to come alive. We watch television, movies, YouTube videos, and plays; we appreciate and relate, and we are more engaged when we connect to the bigger story (Delistraty, 2014). In fact, in his book *The Astonishing Power of Storytelling*, Robert Garmston (2018) cites Cody C. Delistraty (2014), noting that "people remember information when it is weaved into narratives 'up to 22 times more than facts alone'" (p. 3). It is critical that you find something in the story for your colleagues to connect with. When thinking of an impactful story you can tell about the initiative, consider your audience. What do they care about? How might sharing a story about a student whose life could be transformed or a family whose world could change because of this initiative get people to connect?

IDEO U, an online school that focuses on instilling the confidence to pursue creative endeavors and tackle challenges, offers a course called *Storytelling for Influence* (https://bit.ly/2it97ZR). A course like this can help you learn how to tell a story about your work. You may also want to examine George Lakoff and Mark Johnson's (2003) *Metaphors We Live By* or the amazing visual work of Presentation Zen (www .presentationzen.com). Visuals and stories move us—find some that capture the power of your project.

Question 10: Can I Share Data, Evidence, or Research About This Challenge and Decision so Others Will Understand the Need for This Initiative to Move Forward?

Not only do stories have impact; so, too, do numbers. While statistics might not move everyone (statistics about cancer are widely available, but many people still smoke and don't put on sunscreen!), it is helpful to have research to back you up. Does the district have immediate statistics found in journals or academic texts, student testing data or other school data, or results from focus groups? As mentioned previously, you must know the compelling *why* for this project. When working to craft a story with data, getting the data together in ways that those who are new to the initiative can see and understand is key. Easy-to-understand graphics and visuals are critical. The visual marketing site Visually (n.d.) states, "The average human attention span is 8 seconds, and our brains process images 60,000 times faster than text. Infographics make it easier to grab your viewer before the next distraction does."

So add visual data to your presentation if you can. For some inspiration, refer to the work of Edward Tufte (1990), who writes about how visual representation of data makes it easier for those who are looking at it to understand it more deeply. You might have seen data visualization in action on the web. The YouTube video "If the World Were 100 People" (GOOD Magazine, 2017; see https://bit .ly/1YTN8Zq) is a great example of a short visual providing data in a way that allows the viewer to see the data come alive. Visuals can be very compelling.

Question 11: Do I Know and Can I Communicate What My Action Plan Is for Implementation?

We have our story and our data. We now know the *why* and the *what*. Now for the plan. Here's where we come to the *how*.

Before leaders can move forward and lead, it is important to be on the same page with colleagues, working side by side, at the same pace, and with the same understandings. If your colleagues are not on the same page as you and don't understand what the challenge has been, what the decision has come to be, and where they will play their parts in this rollout, holding them accountable isn't going to work. To achieve this common understanding, first, get yourself ready in writing. At some point you will need to create some form of a frequently asked questions (FAQ) communication that will go out in a variety of mediums (for a website, for a staff meeting, and so on). Starting on that FAQ sheet will make it easier to communicate about the rollout in spoken and written form. Following is a set of questions you'll need to have answered and put into an action plan. Some of the responses you need to have at the ready are about how you got here and what is going to happen as you put the decision into action. It is critical to think through all of the responses to these questions before you craft the effective and transparent communication that will take place.

- What challenge are we facing that we want to address? (What story or data can you share to support this?)

- Who was involved in the decision making?

- What process did we use to determine how to address the challenge? (If you weren't involved in the decision, whoever did do the preliminary thinking should share this answer with you for you to share with others.)

- What values undergirded our choices?

- What were the other criteria we considered when we made a decision?

- What was the decision?

- What is the action we will take moving forward? What changes will now take place in classrooms or in the school at large? What specific behaviors do we expect as a result of this initiative coming into being?

- Who will make those changes?

- In what time frame do we need to make those changes?

- What supports will be in place to help those actually implementing the initiative?

- When will those doing the work have an opportunity to evaluate and loop back to review the rollout?

- Who does one talk to if there are concerns?

I have worked with principals who feel they are not the designer of the message but rather the messenger, and they have gotten angry when I suggest they must have answers to these questions as they move forward. "But we don't know the answers," they say. If the district in which you work wants you to support their initiatives, it is incumbent upon *all* involved, from those in central offices to individual schools, to work together to answer these questions for those on the ground who will be implementing changes. We cannot just blame those who work at the district office but instead must work with the district leaders to craft the answers to these questions with those who work there. It is the responsible thing to do.

Question 12: Now That I Have an Action Plan in Place, Do I Know How I Will Communicate This Message?

Once you have a plan for an initiative, and stories, visuals, and data and statistics to support it, provide a strong foundation for communicating the initiative to the right people. How do you communicate it, to whom, and through what media? Deep-end folks don't just put an email out on a Friday afternoon with few details, causing stomachaches for recipients all weekend. Instead, they are mindful of the delivery of the message and consider who needs to know what, and when. You can and should share this information in writing, in person, or in an update to the district office—and continue to do so again and again. It isn't a one-shot press release that is shared and quickly forgotten. It requires revisiting the reasons behind the change and the supports that will continue to be provided, and recognizing the small wins made so far. The research of Hermann Ebbinghaus (1913) established the important role repetition plays in memory. Psychologist Alan Baddeley (1994) confirms its continued relevance, and Sean Kang's (2016) research further supports that spaced repetition promotes effective learning. No doubt you've been annoyed by those commercials on the radio that repeat the name of the pillow or the sleeping pill or whatever product they are selling, and then come back a few times during the broadcast to remind you again! People need to see and hear something several times to get it to stick in their brains—and that isn't just with advertising and marketing, but for a deep-end change in practice too. Additionally, until it is critical and urgent for them, many people don't listen. Remember when cable became the only way to access television in your home? I believe cable providers informed us of the change for eighteen months prior to implementation, and still folks were surprised when their antennas no longer picked up local stations. To ensure the message gets through, leaders should repeat it and make it clear for their team more than they might imagine they'd need to. Put the information into weekly messages, discuss it at professional development sessions, ask that team leads and department chairs to make time for it during meetings. The method can be different, but the reminders of the importance of the initiative should be the same.

Communication of the what and the why is just the beginning. *It is incredibly important when putting an action plan in place to ensure you provide the necessary supports.* Keep mentioning to your team all the training, modeling, or coaching that will be offered. I have seen administrators get angry at staff for not being "on top of things" when they made the decision hastily and then didn't provide the staff with proper preparation time for implementation or training to actually do the work well. And, without the proper support to do it, it will most likely backfire. Mention these supports and the opportunities to utilize them, rather than just focusing on the immediacy of the accountability.

As we'll see more in chapters 2 and 3, there will still be pushback. Table 1.1 offers a list of challenges you might face once you have started rolling out a project, and questions you can answer to build a communication plan that addresses these challenges from the start. If you haven't considered the challenges listed in table 1.1 and communicated your responses to the corresponding questions while you roll out the decision, it can backfire on you. Planning ahead for receiving these questions when you explain the decision regarding the new initiative and being able to articulate answers to the questions in table 1.1 will go a long way in building transparency around the decision itself and, with the supports in place through the school year, implementation will be more successful.

Table 1.1: Challenges and Questions to Address in the Communication Plan

Challenge to Address	Question to Answer in Constructing Your Communication Plan
People will tell you they don't know what to do.	How will you help them gain the knowledge?
People will tell you they don't know how to do it.	How will you help them gain the skills?
People will tell you they don't know why they are doing it.	How will you communicate the rationale?
People will tell you they weren't involved in the decision making.	How will you communicate who was involved in the decision and the reasons for those individuals being at the table?
People will tell you the workload and pressure are increasing too fast.	How will you explain to team members how what they are doing now will change as a result of this new information and what other obligations might, if possible, be taken off their plate in order to focus on this initiative?
People will tell you they don't sense they have support, training, or resources.	Where might staff go for support?
People will tell you they are worried about what will happen if they fail.	How has the school set the culture in terms of innovation and a growth mindset? Has the school been working on a growth mindset for all? Has the school demonstrated support for learning and shared their awareness that implementation dips exist and are expected? If so, can it be reiterated?

Deep-end leaders provide structures for support and accountability and a supportive school environment for all employees to keep things going as smoothly as possible. *Deep-end leaders also don't have hard conversations before they have had clarifying conversations.* If you have been clear about the expectations and the necessary action steps *and* you have been supportive with training and time *and* addressed the answers to the questions in table 1.1 with resources and assistance, then it might be time to hold others accountable—but not before you have offered those supports. If you have been clear and supportive, shared accountability can follow.

Question 13: Am I Aware That There May Be Covert Processes at Work That I Might Not Be Able to Address?

With all this planning, you still might run into unexpected challenges and underlying problems that are difficult to pinpoint—for example, approaching a group and getting the feeling something is happening but you cannot put your finger on it, seeing folks engaging with others when they're out in the parking lot but not in the meeting room, or noticing eye rolls. In these types of experiences, something difficult to identify and describe is alive, but no one discusses it out loud. When I have these experiences, I always think of one of my cognitive crushes, Robert J. Marshak (2006). In his book *Covert Processes at Work: Managing the Five Hidden Dimensions of Organizational Change*, he comments:

> In my experience, things that are overt in work groups tend to be task-related, rational, and defined by the prevailing group norms as legitimate and appropriate in the context. If asked, most members of the group would be aware of and could describe "what is going on." On the other hand, covert processes are more often relationship-related, emotionally based, often . . . unconscious, and defined by the group norms as illegitimate or inappropriate. (p. 46)

Marshak (2006) goes on to explain the concept of covert processes.

> Some typical covert issues in work groups include:
> - Feelings, emotions, and needs regarding power, inclusion, authority, intimacy, attraction, trust, or anger.
> - Fears, taboos, conflicts, and disagreements.
> - Beliefs, norms, and cultural assumptions that guide and limit possibilities. . . .
> - Deals, arrangements, understandings, and "politics." . . .
> - Professional and personal biases and prejudices.
> - Unaddressed or unacknowledged differences based on culture, religion, gender, race, sexual orientation, physical ability, or styles. (pp. 46–47)

You cannot anticipate everything that might bubble up during the communication of the rollout nor should you discuss everything that you notice when things get bumpy during implementation. However, this new learning isn't a get-out-of-jail-free card for deep-end leaders. You cannot now say, "Well, how was I supposed to know there was this undercurrent of resentment from twenty years ago that just surfaced? Oh well," and then just give up. There are many things under the surface that might impact your project and that you might not be able to know are at play. Learn to pay attention and to manage what is unspoken and keep moving forward. For example, in a school I worked in that had a new principal, there was an unspoken undercurrent of resentment by specific teachers that the former principal had favorites. When a new initiative began, the administration explained that one group would be piloting it, and there was immediately a bunch of pushback. Just the word *pilot* brought back memories of favoritism, the thought of some getting favors while others were pushed aside opened old wounds. This example illustrates the need to listen for the language used in a school. Perhaps someone talks about the school's founder even though that person hasn't been in the building for over a decade. Do team members speak nostalgically of "when we had the funds" or of how "when so-and-so was here things were different"? They might not be saying things overtly, but folks are grieving. People may make some digs in passing at "that school" or comments about "those folks" that cause you to recognize power differentials. Pay attention. Then you can try to surface the concerns in safe ways in small groups or one-on-one meetings.

Covert processes are and will be at work. Know they are there, and move on as best as you can with more organizational savvy, understanding, and empathy as you ready for the next bump in the road. I am not suggesting you unearth the covert processes with a flashlight and a shovel, expose them to the light of day, and tell everyone to get over it and move on and expect them to do so. Sometimes the past isn't the past. There is much more to work on, and to work through, and there is a skill to doing so. A deep-end skill. Read Marshak's (2006) book if you are interested in learning more about listening for language and becoming more aware of organizational dynamics. I highly recommend it.

Question 14: Have I Intentionally Designed Stop-And-Reflect Moments Into the Process of Implementation?

When leaders are in the rollout, making headway with their plans, they may often feel a sense of urgency, as they only have so much time to make an impact. However, it's necessary to go slow at certain times to go fast at others. I encourage you to include in your action plan some moments to stop and reflect. As I have witnessed in my twenty years of coaching and consulting, one of the hardest things for many teachers to do is reflect and take time to just sit down and look back on a lesson. It takes courage to recognize what might not have gone as well as you'd hoped, to look at data, to look back, look ahead. It also requires cultivating flexibility and skills.

Educators Maria A. Impedovo and Sufiana Khatoon Malik (2016) agree and state that there is a "need for regular and more guided support in improving reflective practice, especially for junior teachers." It's a common challenge worldwide!

We schedule planning periods but not reflection periods. In the *Harvard Business Review* blog post "Why You Should Make Time for Self-Reflection (Even If You Hate Doing It)," Jennifer Porter (2017) writes:

> Research by Giada Di Stefano, Francesca Gino, Gary Pisano, and Bradley Staats in call centers demonstrated that employees who spent 15 minutes at the end of the day reflecting about lessons learned performed 23% better after 10 days than those who did not reflect.

These data support the idea that if you receive input along the way and you actually reflect on it and change things up, you have a greater chance of improving. This includes having to adjust based on (gulp) negative feedback as well as just making small course corrections. It helps to remember these words from Stone and Heen (2014): "Others' views of you are input, not imprint." (p. 182). This can be difficult when, with all the effort you've put forth, you just want to do the work and not think about changing it. It can be exhausting because sometimes the changes sting.

In my book *Hard Conversations Unpacked* (Abrams, 2016), I include a few ideas to help overcome fears surrounding gaining and reflecting on feedback.

- Ritualize it; do it consistently. When you work in an iterative manner, you are always adjusting and always growing. It gets easier when you can think of gathering feedback as just one step in the rollout. Processing feedback and making improvements is just working on the next iteration. It isn't going to be a final draft.

- Before you begin a reflection moment you expect to be difficult, ground yourself. Take two deep breaths—breathe in for a count of six, hold for a count of three, and breathe out. The focus on getting oxygen into your body, which with shallow breathing doesn't happen as easily, will help you become more calm, centered, and energized.

- Remember that people of different cultures and backgrounds listen and give feedback differently. Be understanding when feedback you receive comes at you in a way that isn't your style.

- Friend failure; don't become it. I have heard many people say, "I'm such a failure." You, yourself, do not *equate to failure*. Be wary of labeling yourself.

- If you are taken by surprise, take two deep breaths. Get oxygen to your brain. By concentrating on breathing, you put yourself in the moment with more energy to offer to the situation.

- If you are concerned you are going to get emotional, either with anger or tears, I have been told not to look down. In my experience, looking down moves you into a mental space where you will feel emotions more strongly. What works for me is to instead look up; it takes me to a more neutral space so I am less focused on emotions.

- If you are feeling a bit out of control, sip some water or coffee to give yourself a second to get your brain in a space to respond. Bring a bottle of water to hold during the reflection meeting and grab it often. It will ground you.

- When someone says, "Can I give you some feedback?" Say, "I am open to feedback and respond best when it is humane and growth producing." It will most likely stop them from saying something that is too off the cuff or unkind.

As mentioned at the beginning of this section, deep-end leaders may feel a sense of urgency, as they only have so much time to make an impact, and some may not consider reflection to be forward movement. However, remember that we must sometimes go slow to go fast. Plan reflection time to gather input during the roll out. Get yourself ready to listen, and then do so. Deep-end leaders who are worried about the emotional overload this might have can look forward to chapter 4 (page 67), which focuses on the fourth foundational skill, managing yourself through change and resistance.

Conclusion

Deep-end leaders have a strategy for each aspect of thinking before you speak and support others in the process as well. It takes cognitive ability and emotional intelligence to think before you speak and to work with others to make an initiative come to life. Consistency, communication, and transparency will help team members take ownership of the decisions that have been put in place for the initiative and make the process easier. Increasing one's cognitive ability to address these types of questions for each project you are working with is an ongoing practice for deep-enders—and one I believe Adam Grant would applaud. In the next chapter, we move on to what many leaders have asked me for—ways to manage resistance when the initiative has been announced. On to the social-skill building.

Reflection Questions

Wade into the following questions for team or individual reflection.

- As you look at the self-assessment questions for thinking before you speak, where do you need some extra attention or focus in order to be well prepared? What more do you need to think about?

- How might supervisors or central office colleagues support you to be even more effective with a rollout at your site? Is there a question or two from this chapter that you might ask them about?

CHAPTER 2

Preempting Resistance

Organizations don't change. People do—or they don't.
—Rick Torben

Even when you have worked diligently at thinking-before-you-speak planning, expect that you will still meet resistance. It is normal that adults will have concerns about the project. It's understandable they'd be anxious or curious about how this new work might affect them. Even if the challenge they will come up against is exciting and welcome and the initiative is something they want to embrace, the change will likely trigger anxieties about what they will need to do differently. In order to preempt resistance, deep-end leaders must maintain awareness of their team members' anxieties and concerns.

Robert Garmston, co-author with Art Costa (Costa & Garmston, 2015) of *Cognitive Coaching*, helped me see that this type of other-focused awareness has a name. When we are looking at a situation from another's point of view, we are being more *allocentric*: not self-focused (egocentric) but other-focused. Allocentric. Anticipating others' concerns with an allocentric mindset will help you preempt resistance and collaborate on the initiative a bit more smoothly.

I learned the most about collaboration from two books: (1) *Radical Collaboration* by James W. Tamm and Ronald J. Luyet (2005) and (2) *How the Way We Talk Can Change the Way We Work* by Robert Kegan and Lisa Laskow Lahey (2001). Imagining that collaboration was all about talking and working with *other* people, I was surprised that the first half of both books talk about *you*. No other person is even mentioned for the first half of each text. It is all about how you talk to yourself and how self-aware you are. In the end, effective collaboration starts with you.

But isn't this book about being in the deep end with regard to a given initiative and how to get *others* on board? Isn't this chapter about how to get a head start on managing the resistance that will come your way during the rollout? While all of that is true, and I will get to the main point of preempting resistance, we must start with the Ancient Greek aphorism: know thyself. In knowing oneself, it will be easier to understand what triggers you when you manage the resistance others will have. A *trigger* is generally understood as a stimulus that causes anxiety, and resistance from others could be that stimulus. Or, as mentioned in question 13 from the last chapter, just some words spoken about the initiative might set off something inside us and cause us to respond in an unhelpful way. No matter what *trigger* means to you, if we can preempt something that will cause unhelpful anxiety we are better off. Because there will be resistance. And how *you* show up matters.

This chapter focuses on knowing yourself in order to then better know the adults you are working with on an initiative. Reviewing the self-assessment questions on preempting resistance will help build this social intelligence and shine a light on the needs of others so when you get into the work that supports students, it goes more smoothly. Know thyself, yes. But know others too. Deep-enders do both.

Know Thyself

So, let's begin with some questions that will help us review the essential skill of knowing thyself. Your answers to these questions will help you recognize that you, too, show up every day with needs and concerns that shape how you wish others to communicate with you. It can also help you see and serve as a reminder of how others' preferences may differ. The action plan you set out for a new initiative might be right up your alley, but it might *not* be at all how someone else likes to work. What you think is the right way to do one's job isn't the same for others. You personally might thrive on new learning and be totally okay with interruptions to your work, and this new initiative seems fun for you given that it will be a learning curve with lots of stops and starts, but your colleague hates all this newness and uncertainty. Responding to the following list of questions Jennifer Abrams and Valerie von Frank (2014) offer can help you begin to develop this awareness:

- Are you a "get things done right away" or a "give me a day or two to think about it" kind of worker?

- Which tasks do you enjoy doing with others? Which tasks do you feel better doing on your own?

- What are your strengths as a worker? What about as a co-worker? What do you feel are your learning edges?

- What motivates you at work?
- What situations/challenges/work assignments do you find fun? Which ones challenge you?
- How do you handle interruptions or a change of plans? How might someone work best with you in those types of situations?
- Do you consider yourself an introvert or an extrovert? In which situations?
- If you have taken any other personality/work style/learning style assessment, what learnings might be useful to share with others?
- What are the best ways to communicate with you? Text, email, in person, phone?
- Do you tend to write in brief or be detailed? What types of direction do you need when you go off and do an assignment? A bulleted list of to dos with deadlines or just the gist of what is to be done?
- How will others know you are hurt or upset? If you are upset, how do you want to be treated?
- How do like to handle mistakes? Yours or others?
- In a group situation, what are your strengths? What can you be counted on for? Keeping others on track, always bringing in another perspective?
- What types of acknowledgements do you like? Public or private praise, tangible gifts, etc.
- In what situations do you ask for help? How do you feel about asking for help?
- How would you like to receive feedback? In what forms?
- What are your pet peeves in terms of team work/working with others/collaborating?
- Do you consider yourself a risk taker? In what areas of your life do you like to be spontaneous? In others where are you more cautious?
- How much of your personal life do you like to share with those at work?
- Are you someone who socializes with colleagues from work? Lunch with those while at work? (p. 77)

Knowing yourself helps you see what might trigger you about others' reactions as they speak out when the rollouts begin and allows you to anticipate what reactions might irritate you, so you can better plan to respond in a productive way. And people will resist the rollout. Don't freak out. Knowing where you freak out the most is a good start to preempting resistance that others will bring your way.

Additional "Know Thyself" Resources

- Myers-Briggs Type Indicator (www.myersbriggs.org)
- Strengths Finder (www.strengthsfinder.com/home.aspx)
- True Colors (https://truecolorsintl.com)
- VIA Survey of Character Strengths (www.viacharacter.org/www)
- The New Science of Team Chemistry: Pioneers, Drivers, Integrators, and Guardians (https://hbr.org/2017/03/the-new-science-of-team-chemistry)

Know Others

Now that we have done a self-study and reviewed what might trigger us and challenge us in understanding others and their concerns with the rollout of this initiative, we are ready to go even further in building our social intelligence. To begin, let's consider the list of questions from Abrams and von Frank (2014; see pages 40–41) in connection with how others might perceive this new initiative and how it aligns with how they prefer to work. Do you know what might trigger them about this new initiative and its action plan? Upon hearing the news of this new initiative coming to their classrooms, many will find themselves triggered and could start to resist, either passively or actively. Perhaps they don't take interruptions well; they like to work alone, and this initiative requires them to share their room and co-teach; or they like to take a day or two to think, and this initiative puts them in short meetings that require immediate answers. Their communication and learning styles don't align with what it takes to roll out this initiative as is. Deep-end leaders know how to pick up on clues. Ask yourself the following questions.

- "Am I attentive to the emotional cues others give me?"
- "Do I listen well? Not just to ready myself to respond, but to truly understand?"
- "Do I know my colleagues' strengths and accomplishments?"

- "Do I understand the power structures at play in my organization and how others might see them differently?"

- "Do I show sensitivity for and understanding of my colleagues' perspectives?"

- "Do I respect and relate well to my colleagues from a variety of backgrounds and those who hold different perspectives than mine (culture, politics, beliefs, and so on)?"

- "Do I understand diverse worldviews, communicate with sensitivity, and appreciate differences?"

- "Do I challenge myself in terms of where I have bias and can be intolerant?"

I have a colleague who took several years learning about his faculty before he made the decision to roll out specific initiatives as he was aware of the cues he was getting. While he was in a position of authority for those couple of years and could have mandated change, he also knew that mandating something wouldn't be the way to go given the sense of autonomy the faculty had grown accustomed to. He built up a structure of support within the school over time and then brought to the school a new way of doing specific tasks. It wasn't fast, but it was more successful because he was sensitive to the dynamics of the group. Your social intelligence and self-awareness can be tremendous assets in making this rollout a success.

You might be saying at this point, "All this study of the other adults feels like misplaced energy. You are talking about meeting the needs of the adults and it should be all about the students." Ah, that polarity management rears its head again. It has to be about both. In order to move to the work of the school, we must consider the needs of those who work within it.

A Plug for the National School Reform Faculty

The National School Reform Faculty (www.nsrfharmony.org) is masterful at bringing colleagues together in humane and supportive ways to find out how others think, feel, and act. Its week-long workshops in how to become a Critical Friends Group facilitator are good professional learning opportunities. Even if you haven't taken one of its workshops, you have no doubt been in a team-building workshop where the facilitators put you in N, E, S, W quadrants of a room to show how we all come to a task with a different way of moving forward. Norths believe in acting (let's do it), East people want to speculate (look at the big picture), Souths believe everyone's feelings should be taken into consideration, and Wests believe in detail (know the who, what, and when). There are strengths and limitations to each. There are aspects we value and aspects that drive us crazy in the other quadrants. But we are all in it together, and deep-end leaders must be allocentric and other-focused and not believe that those with other ways of looking at the work have moral defects. We need to work together. If you not familiar with the National School Reform Faculty's work, I urge you to visit www.nsrfharmony.org now to learn more.

The more I work with others on deep-end communication the more I understand how important it is for all people to be seen as individuals, and to have others understand who we are and how we got here. At the risk of repeating the word too often, deep-end leaders need to understand this psychological need to be seen in a deep way. We need to be consistently asking, "What might someone we work with be thinking about this work? How might they feel in this situation?" And when it comes to the resistance that others might offer in response to change in general and our initiative specifically, this awareness comes in handy.

So, in a hard conversation (a deep-end thing to do) or in any possibly stressful interaction (parent-teacher conference, supervisory discussion, or, in the case of this book, the rollout of an initiative), we need to be even *more* allocentric. Consider your colleagues in relation to your deep-end initiative, and ask yourself the following questions. Thinking about the answers to these questions ahead of time can provide you with a chance to frame the conversation and choose words wisely.

- "What are their past experiences with changes in your organization or school?"

- "What are their current realities? What else is going on at this time?"

- "Are they experiencing any personal or family challenges at this time? Are they caregivers? Dealing with young families? Might these personal factors take more of their mental and emotional energy at this juncture?"

- "Is anyone currently managing a mental health challenge?"

- "Are they from a different generation than yours? If so, might this give them a different take on this project and its implementation? Without stereotyping, might they see things differently based on their history and age?"

- "Are there race, culture, or country of origin factors here that you need to not only acknowledge but better understand in particular connection to the initiative and its content?"

- "Are there socioeconomic differences you need to take into account as you consider their points of view?"

- "Are there gender differences that could be at play?"

- "Are there spiritual values or religious beliefs you need to consider?"

When I think about specific initiatives—for example, support for English learners, trauma sensitivity, a focus on special needs (poverty, learning challenges, and so on), a social-emotional learning curriculum, a more structured literacy or mathematics curriculum, or an intervention push-in program—knowing how your colleagues might see those projects is critical in understanding their needs during the rollout and implementation. I have seen conflict around a change in approaching discipline from more traditional work to more of a restorative justice approach. I have heard of push and pull around detracking, and the cognitive tussle had origins in the upbringings of those involved in implementing in the initiative. In the case of detracking, there might be one person who had been taught in a school with tracked classes in which she felt comfortable and in which she felt success, and so in her current school she continues to advocate grouping students in a way that made sure students identified as "accelerated" had some focused time. Another might have had a different experience in his home country where the community placed all students together to learn and did not track students. He felt that being in classes with students of all abilities and talents was a terrific way to teach. Yet others from rural areas with home schooling and online learning may have grown up with more personalized learning from the get-go and have another perspective. Knowing a bit more about who we are working with helps us understand points of view they might bring to the work they do.

A Deep Dive Into Self-Assessment Questions

You should have already completed the deep-end self-assessment around your initiative or project in the introduction (figure I.2, pages 9–11). In the remainder of this chapter, we will reflect on questions from your deep-end self-assessment that focus on the second of the four foundational deep-end skills—preempting resistance—and determine for which questions you have a learning edge.

Question 1: Do I Know What Questions and Concerns Most Commonly Come Up With a New Initiative and How I Might Address Them Early in the Rollout Process?

As I said in chapter 1, and I will reiterate again, I am a big believer in the idea of pacing before leading. Get in sync with your colleagues *before* you move ahead. If you are hoping someone will get on board with a given initiative, he or she needs to understand what the change in behavior is supposed to look like and sound like, because holding people accountable for something they don't understand to begin with isn't going to work. As consultant Blaine Lee, author of *The Power Principle* (1997) has said, "Almost all conflict is a result of violated expectations" (as cited in Covey, 2008, p. 198). There needs to be a clarifying conversation before any account-ability can or should take place. Table 2.1 lists some common concerns leaders should be prepared to face when introducing a new initiative, and types of clarifying conver-sations they can plan to address those concerns and preempt resistance.

Table 2.1: Common Concerns and Clarifying Conversations

Concern	Clarifying Conversation
We don't understand this idea enough.	Clear communication about the training that will take place or the information to be provided
We don't know how to do it in practice.	Communication about the training that will take place and the modeling and the coaching that will be provided
Why are we doing this again?	Communication about the rationale (evidence, data, and so on)
Who was involved in this plan? No one asked me.	Communication about who was involved in the decision and the reasons for those individuals being at the table
The workload is already too much to handle and there are too many initiatives already. What are you taking off my plate?	Communication of what we are doing now and what might be coming off their plates
Who is in charge of this? Whom can I go to for answers? Who is involved in the support of this initiative?	Communication of who are in these roles and when they will be available for support
We have seen things like this come and go. And how many months do we have to implement this? What if it doesn't work? What are the repercussions?	Reiteration about growth mindsets and the culture of innovation; clear articulation of time lines; communication; clear articulation of how individuals will be held accountable

While it is frustrating for many of us who know the initiative, its rationale, and its plan inside and out to have to keep explaining the answers to these questions, they will come up in some form or another, regardless of the initiative. Being ready to respond helps you calmly preempt the resistance.

Question 2: Do I Know the People I Am Working With in Some Personal Way?

Knowing our students and their backgrounds is essential in the work we do in the classroom. How we welcome all students and understand how their home lives impact their learning is part and parcel of what we do as good educators. Knowing our adult learners and where they are coming from is also essential. Individuals bring their whole selves to work—their worries, their challenges, and their understandings of what work and school should be and how they play a role. Knowing who is in your building and how their personal lives integrate with their professional work is key. Knowing how different faculty members might see your initiative given their backgrounds is useful if you want to preempt resistance. The following list (not exhaustive, but a start) of factors influencing educators' identities gives us a starting point to think about who we are working with and how they will see the projects we are hoping to roll out.

- Seniority
- Role or position
- Immigration status
- Place of origin
- Citizenship
- Creed or religion
- Family status
- Marital status
- Caregiving responsibilities
- Socioeconomic status
- Level of education
- English language ability
- Geographic location
- Ancestry
- Race
- Age
- Physical ability
- Ethnicity
- Biological gender
- Gender identity
- Sexual orientation

Are you rolling out an initiative that will take three to five years to get underway? Do you have a significant population of employees who plan on retiring in the next two to three years? Will the work required for this new project require some out-of-town seminars that may affect young parents or other caregivers on your staff? Do you plan on doing something that will push people to communicate up and down the institutional hierarchy in a more collaborative way, and do you have group members from cultures that look at status and roles as more top down? Knowing who you are working with is key to anticipating such concerns.

When it comes to who we are as teaching staff, we might do well to look at social psychologist Geert Hofstede's work on cultural differences (www.geert-hofstede.com). Hofstede and colleagues (Hofstede, Hofstede, & Minkov, 2010) conducted one of the most comprehensive studies of how culture influences values in the workplace. Hofstede et al. (2010) write about six different dynamics that one might face across cultures and that could impact the work environment. We are all raised within a culture that, for lack of a better word, "sides with" one side or another on these poles, and if the initiative in the school falls on the other side of the polarity than an individual is accustomed to, it could cause some anxiety and resistance. Here are the six polarities.

1. **Power distances:** Was the culture you grew up in more hierarchical and unequal, or was it more flat and united?

2. **Individual or collective:** Was the culture you grew up in more about focusing on you and your family, or focusing on community?

3. **Masculine or feminine:** Does the culture you grew up in value more of an assertive (masculine) culture, or was it more cooperative (feminine)?

4. **Uncertainty or avoidance:** Was the culture you grew up in OK with ambiguity (uncertainty), or was it more rules focused (avoidance)?

5. **Long-term or shot-term orientation:** Does the culture you grew up in have a more traditional lens of keeping things as-is, or was it open to change at a faster pace?

6. **Indulgence or restraint:** Was the culture you grew up in OK with pleasure, or did it advocate control and restraint?

Think about how differences within these polarities might influence your team or staff. These are polarities and there is no right answer, but imagine where your initiative falls on the continuum and who might have reservations. The initiative might go against how they see the world and cause some friction for you and for them.

You might also view these moments of difference through the frame of polarity management. As explained in the previous chapter, polarities are coexisting circumstances that require a *yes, and* rather than an *either-or* approach (Kise, 2014). Framing the initiative in terms of helping everyone get a little more balanced in the center versus tipping the proverbial seesaw all the way to the other side might help you preempt some resistance. Imagine how your initiative might be framed as managing a polarity or opening the aperture to discover a new way of looking at the world.

Table 2.2 includes some common initiatives schools might roll out that may meet resistance based on team members' cultural polarities. Contemplate how these new projects might meet resistance from your colleagues if they have a different take on what schools should be focusing on through either of these frames. Remember that these are differences in how to view the world—not right and wrong ways, but different frames.

Table 2.2: Possible Initiatives Resulting in Resistance Based on Polarity

Polarity	Initiatives That Might Meet Resistance
Power Distance We see the world as hierarchical and there is inequality we must deal with.	Detracking students Opening up gifted and talented classes to all students Practicing inclusion Working on growth versus fixed mindsets
Individualism and Collectivism We care for ourselves and our families most of all.	Fundraising done districtwide, not just school by school Teaching sex education
Masculine and Feminine We prefer achievement, assertiveness, and material rewards for success.	Engaging in restorative justice, co-teaching, and social-emotional learning programs
Uncertainty-Avoidance We feel uncomfortable with uncertainty and ambiguity. We need to control the future with rigid codes of belief and behavior.	Using project-based learning and personalized learning
Long-Term Orientation Versus Short-Term Normative Orientation We prefer to maintain time-honored traditions and norms while viewing societal change with suspicion.	Having service learning requirements Offering internships Using senior exhibitions or portfolios Using project-based learning
Indulgence Versus Restraint We are okay with gratification of basic and natural human drives related to enjoying life and having fun.	Changing summer school requirements, truancy policies, or graduation requirements

Source: Hofstede et al., 2010.

Question 3: Am I Aware of Adult Learning Theory and How It Might Connect to the Initiative I Am Implementing?

One of my favorite teachers who focuses on adult learning is Professor Emeritus Linda Lambert of California State University, East Bay. Of all the work she has done on the subject, the following three essential pieces need to be in our planning as we work with adults changing course (Lambert et al., 2002). Consider how these concepts relate to your initiative and how can you modify your plan and language in order to work with them and preempt resistance.

1. **Adults have a drive toward competence, which is linked to self-image and efficacy:** We all want to feel competent and in control. It is embarrassing to perceive that you are being told that what you have been doing is wrong and even more frustrating to see yourself as ineffective. How can you add awareness of this concern to your communications? What alignment can you make between what has been done before that works and what is happening now? What do folks already know, what can they build on or adjust, and what might they have to completely scrap and start on from scratch? And what type of control will they have so they feel they have choices and autonomy? Making sure to mention what is going great, and what won't change, using the words such as *expertise*, *capacity*, *options*, and *suggestions* all indicate to the listeners that the speaker sees their strengths and acknowledges their need for ownership and choice.

2. **Learning is both an opportunity and a risk; it requires dissonance and change:** Carol Dweck's book *Mindset: The New Psychology of Success* (2006) speaks to her research on building a growth mindset as essential in our efforts with students, and we need to live with a growth mindset as adults as well. Leaders can encourage growth mindsets by repeating aloud an acknowledgement that new projects are risky, one might not get it right the first time, and that they are aware there are rough drafts, iterations, and discomfort for adults as well, and it's okay. Challenge is fun. Learning comes from it not working right the first time, and discomfort isn't bad. These ideas should be stated over and over.

   The Hasso Plattner Institute of Design at Stanford (https://dschool .stanford.edu), Ewan MacIntosh's NoTosh consultancy (https://notosh .com) and many others bring the ideas of growth mindset, creative problem solving, and failing forward into their work on design thinking. Everything is an iteration, not a final draft. If we build up a growth mindset where challenge and continuous learning are part and parcel of how we all move ahead, and expect iterations, we will be in a better place to move forward with less discomfort in our psyches and in our communities. And your community might not live in that ecosystem just yet. Change in small doses is okay, but for many folks continuous change is not. Be mindful about the psychological cost of dissonance.

3. **Learning is the continual process of identity formation, or growing into more of who we are becoming:** My former superintendent Kevin Skelly was speaking in front of eight hundred employees on the opening day of school in his first year in Palo Alto Unified School District. He unabashedly said to us all, "I woke up this morning and said to myself, 'Hot dang. I am the sup'" (K. Skelly, personal communication, August, 2008). We were all a bit taken aback. Our leader, the person who is in charge, was himself kind of surprised by his job title. It was a new one for him, and he was still forming his identity. We thought he already *was* the superintendent, and in title he was, but *inside* he was growing into that role. People tend to not be very generous with the adults they work with in this respect; we want them already fully formed. I think that is a truly unrealistic expectation given the innovation and rapid change that is taking place and the demands we face in schools. We have to allow for the identity formation of both the adults and the students if we want to keep our profession moving in an upward trajectory.

To preempt resistance, consider how all three of these adult learning concepts can connect to how you message your initiative, how you speak to the accountability around it, and how you stay as allocentric as you can while the initiative moves ahead.

Question 4: Do I Understand the Psychological Threat-or-Reward Instinct so I Can Mitigate Fears During My Communications?

Neuropsychologist David Rock (2008, 2009) studies how comments in conversation can produce a fight-or-flight response in the other party. According to Rock, (2008), a person engaged in a conversation immediately evaluates whether it is a situation in which he or she feels safe and wants to engage, and if the conversation is going to be worthwhile. The person also evaluates whether the interaction will cause him or her to feel positively or negatively about him- or herself. Rock (2008) calls this a threat-or-reward instinct, and it is pervasive in personal interactions, including professional learning communities, performance reviews, and in the rollout of initiatives. Deep-end thinkers are mindful as to whether listeners will feel threatened or rewarded when faced with the new project.

Rock's (2008) SCARF model can support your language surrounding the implementation process to improve the outcome of threat-or-reward scenarios. SCARF is an acronym Rock (2008) uses for the five psychological triggers we experience in an interaction that either diminish us or create safety: (1) status, (2) certainty, (3) autonomy, (4) relatedness, and (5) fairness. Rock (2008) describes the SCARF model in the following way:

> The SCARF model involves five domains of human social experience: Status, Certainty, Autonomy, Relatedness and Fairness. . . . These five domains activate either the "primary reward" or "primary threat" circuitry (and associated networks) of the brain. (p. 44)

This model can support deep-end leaders in designing personalized communication action plans that are mindful of the threat-reward schema and lessen the potential for team members to feel threatened during interactions around an initiative implementation.

As you think about who you are working with and the initiative you will be rolling out, consider in what ways this change might make individuals feel threatened and then use the ideas from the SCARF model to make them feel less threatened. The following list offers guidance for considering each element of the SCARF model.

- **Status:** This refers to the importance of one's self compared to others. For your initiative, consider acknowledging the following.
    - How long someone has been on staff
    - What roles he or she has played while on staff
    - The expertise he or she has (including degrees, awards, and so on)
- **Certainty:** This refers to the ability to predict the future. For your initiative, consider how you might learn about and acknowledge the following.

- What specifically the person will need to change in his or her practice
- What the next steps will be in order to implement the initiative with fidelity

- **Autonomy:** This refers to having some control over one's environment or actions. In this initiative, consider how you might learn about and acknowledge the following.
  - What one can do his or her way and what he or she should do in a uniform way
  - What the time frame is for getting it done and what won't work
  - What someone can do or not do successfully

- **Relatedness:** This refers to belonging and connection. In this initiative, acknowledge the following.
  - What this initiative means for the people in the school
  - How they will do the work together as a community and as a team

- **Fairness:** This refers to having the same rules and processes for everyone. In this initiative, acknowledge the following.
  - If the initiative is only meant for specific departments or teams, why it isn't the same for everyone and what the reason is for that inequity
  - How the initiative aligns with their contract and stated standards

Being linguistically savvy and mindful of psychological needs are key. It is a sure bet that these threat-or-reward interactions and moments trigger your colleagues, and you too. Folks have asked me, "What if you don't know who has which need? I have 120 people I am working with. It is impossible to be aware of all of their individual concerns." One gentleman asked me how he was going to actually get the work done with all of this awareness of others thrown in. He had an initiative to manage. Being mindful of your wording is a good start. How about acknowledging *all* needs and most likely addressing everyone in that way? How about articulating an appreciation for veterans and newcomers? How about emphasizing certain specifics and opportunities for individual choice? How about addressing the need for connection as team members move forward and need each other's assistance as they each take on a piece of the work? That way you are attempting to acknowledge all needs.

Question 5: Am I Mindful That Others Are at Different Developmental Stages in Their Own Growth and That I Need to Communicate With Them Differently? How Might This Initiative Challenge Them, and How Might I Support Them to Move Forward With the Initiative?

Deep-end educators know that they must adjust their communications to be better understood and to get their messages across effectively. Consider how your initiative might challenge different people and how you might support them to move forward. The work of Ellie Drago-Severson and Jessica Blum-DeStefano (2016) best reflects this thinking about how a person might hear you best. In their book *Tell Me So I Can Hear You*, which I strongly encourage you to read, they speak of four ways of knowing: (1) instrumental (rule-based), (2) socialized (other-focused), (3) self-authoring (reflective), and (4) self-transforming (interconnecting). These ways of knowing are not fixed or hierarchical; they are situational and contextual. The idea is that recognizing how another person might receive you in a conversation based on their way of knowing will help you consider how to best pitch your ideas to ensure your points are heard.

Table 2.3 describes Drago-Severson and Blum-DeStefano's (2016) ways of knowing and suggests what you might need to emphasize about your initiative in order to be successful with a variety of people.

Table 2.3: Developmental Ways of Knowing

Way of Knowing	Teacher Concerns	Think About Emphasizing
Instrumental Way of Knowing	If the administrator uses big-picture language, I will be confused and irritated, as I need concrete next steps. If he or she doesn't give me the most specific details that affect me personally, I will be anxious.	Include concrete suggestions, models, and rule-based examples.
Socialized Way of Knowing	If this rollout is going to criticize how I have been doing it, I won't like it. Appreciate my effort. It's all in how you engage me in this rollout. Authority figures are right, but I need you to be nice to me as you teach me about the rollout.	Add in appreciation for effort and contribution. Validate progress.

Self-Authoring Way of Knowing	Confirming autonomy will be the way to get me to listen. Offer me options and ideas and allow me to self-assess how this will help me move toward a bigger goal I have. Stretch my brain by having me work with others to explore additional ways to work.	Keep your eye on the idea of autonomy and offer opportunities to add in the person's ideas and develop his or her next reflective steps. Provide opportunities to collaboratively reflect on practice and explore alternatives, contradictions, and paradoxes. Think in terms of the big picture and how a change in behavior can move the person toward a greater goal.
Self-Transforming Way of Knowing	We are all involved in the rollout and continual design of the implementation process. I think we should embrace the complexity of the challenge. If it is too simple, it is too simple.	Provide opportunities to collaboratively reflect on practice and explore alternatives, contradictions, and paradoxes.

Source: Adapted from Drago-Severson & Blum-DeStefano, 2016, p. 65.

Conclusion

This entire chapter is like a kaleidoscope of ways to look at those with whom you work and consider in what ways they might find the initiative you are hoping to roll out be a bit too problematic. In this chapter, I have offered introductions to frames and allocentric ways to approach resistance with awareness. From SCARF to ways of knowing, from cultural differences to mindfulness around identity, you can look at this initiative and your colleagues' concerns through many filters. If you wish to swim in the deep end, you will need to keep these ways of knowing in mind. An allocentric mindset takes you a long way, and yet, resistance remains. Chapter 3 helps you manage your voice when responding to that resistance.

Reflection Questions

Wade into the following questions for team or individual reflection.

- In the Know Thyself section, where were your learning edges that might impact your ability to roll out your initiative successfully?

- Which question from this portion of the deep-end self-assessment caused the most self-reflection?

- What are your next steps in terms of learnings to help preempt resistance that will come your way?

CHAPTER 3

Responding to Resistance

What we need more than anything else is not textbooks but text people.
—Abraham Joshua Heschel

Even when we attempt to understand others and are allocentric in our thinking to plan for resistance, we must still prepare for how to respond to resistant behaviors when they occur. This requires the key skills of exercising control in the moment and managing impulsivity when others have not. As Heschel (1953) implies in the chapter epigraph, we don't need to just read about how to accomplish this, we need to live it. I am in agreement. Count me in. Textbooks are good to read. Text people are great to emulate.

Managing oneself and not allowing personal frustrations to come out in negative ways is an ongoing struggle. Deep-end leaders need to understand that others will be triggered and, in response, they need to *respond*, not *react*. This involves:

- Dealing with difficult issues in a straightforward way, without placing blame

- Being able to take negative feedback and listen without reacting with defensiveness and blame

- Monitoring the intensity of one's responses

These are all key learnings for a deep-end leader. This chapter gives you a start in how to build up your verbal and nonverbal agility so when others react you do not impulsively react back. First, we'll look at linguistic norms necessary for successful collaboration, and then examine the self-assessment questions for responding to resistance in detail to help you gauge your strengths and weaknesses with each item.

Finally, we'll explore strategies to help deep-end leaders more successfully respond to resistance.

The Seven Norms of Collaborative Work

The social ecosystem in which educators live and work should have some basic agreements, no matter what, about how to relate to each other and how the school community functions and communicates. Many of us have credentials in how to work effectively with students, but never learned how to talk and work effectively with adults. There has to be a foundational set of norms for communication. In this book, I focus on linguistic norms. For additional resources on professionalism and the norms around that concept that extend out of the verbal realm, please see Resource A: Extended List of Professional Teacher Behaviors in *Having Hard Conversations* (Abrams, 2009).

Garmston and Bruce Wellman (1999) propose seven linguistic norms as the base from which all work in schools is done.

1. **Pausing:** Pausing before responding or asking a question allows time for thinking and enhances dialogue, discussion, and decision making.

2. **Paraphrasing:** Using a paraphrase starter that is comfortable for you, such as "So . . ." or "As you are . . ." or "You're thinking . . ." and following the starter with a paraphrase assists members of the group to hear and understand each other as they formulate questions.

3. **Posing questions:** Using gentle, open-ended probes or inquiries such as "Please say more . . ." or "I'm curious about . . ." or "I'd like to hear more about . . ." or "Then, are you saying . . . ?" increases the clarity and precision of the group's thinking.

4. **Putting ideas on the table:** Ideas are at the heart of meaningful dialogue. Label the intention of your comments. For example, you might say, "Here is one idea . . ." or "One thought I have is . . ." or "Here is a possible approach . . . ."

5. **Providing data:** Providing data, both qualitative and quantitative, in a variety of forms supports group members in constructing shared understanding from their work. Data have no meaning beyond that which we make of them; shared meaning develops from collaboratively exploring, analyzing, and interpreting data.

6. **Paying attention to self and others:** Meaningful dialogue follows when each group member is conscious of the self and of others and is aware of not only what he or she is saying but also of how he or she says it and how others are responding. This includes paying attention to learning style when planning for, facilitating, and participating in group meetings. Responding to others in their own language forms is one manifestation of this norm.

7. **Presuming positive intentions:** Assuming that others' intentions are positive promotes and facilitates meaningful dialogue and eliminates unintentional put-downs. Using positive intentions in your speech is one manifestation of this norm.

Think about whether you live out these norms in your meetings. Do you use these norms on a daily basis in your interactions? Knowing how to communicate with intention in collaborative groups is the foundation from which new work can take hold and new initiatives can roll out with greater ease.

Having norms for how we talk to each other is essential. It forms the social contract we have with one another that governs how we interact on a daily basis. We can put this set of linguistic norms in place so that when we introduce an initiative and people resist that change, we have a base from which we can better respond to that resistance without defensiveness and blame.

A Deep Dive Into Self-Assessment Questions

You should have already completed the deep-end self-assessment around your initiative or project in the introduction (see figure I.2, pages 9–11). In the remainder of this chapter, we will reflect on questions from your deep-end self-assessment that focus on the third of the four foundational deep-end skills (responding to resistance), determine for which questions you have a learning edge, and consider strategies for responding to resistance.

Question 1: Given That Resistance Will Happen, Do I Know Ways I Can Respond Professionally to Those Who Respond Negatively to the Initiative?

Even if you have addressed in your communications the fear of change that chapters 1 and 2 brought up, people will still push as their SCARF model threats come to the fore, their adult learning needs remain unmet, or they see things differently. And they might not be as gracious with their communications of frustration as you'd like.

A deep-end leader doesn't go low and respond with anger or frustration but instead attempts to respond with professionalism. Following are a few ideas on how to manage resistance and respond in different situations with linguistic savvy, adapted from *Hard Conversations Unpacked* (Abrams, 2016). See if they apply in your contexts.

- **If someone intimidates you by shouting, name-calling, swearing, or threatening:** "You have every right to feel that way, but no right to express it in an offensive manner. Please restate your objection in a more polite way."

- **If someone responds using words like *never, always,* or *every time* instead of talking about a specific situation:** "While it may seem true that this happens 'all the time' or that I never respond, the truth is that is not true. It is an over-generalization. Let's try to focus the conversation on this specific situation."

- **If someone bring things up from the past that have nothing to do with the present rollout:** "I understand that there were experiences prior to this one that you feel have a connection with what we are talking about. At this point, that information isn't the focus of this *current* conversation and implementation. Let's direct our attention to this *specific* rollout."

- **If someone wants to be let off the hook in rolling out this initiative:** "Everyone is responsible for this implementation. While I understand your circumstances [share details], I also understand the need for all parties to do the rollout. What can I do to support you, because I am committed to making sure the work is done?"

- **If someone says, "The way this is being handled assumes we aren't professionals":** "Many professions, ours included, have standards and are constantly held accountable to changing expectations and the newest research. Think about doctors and tax accountants and pilots. They are held responsible to doing the work in alignment with the latest findings or policies. Professionals hold each other accountable to doing what is best practice. And holding ourselves up to standards is research based so we need to go forward."

- **If someone says, "The district always makes us . . .":** "We are the district. All of us. I am included. If you are talking about the district office, that is another discussion and yet we each have a voice. We can always ask our colleagues for clarification, seek support, and ask that those working there address concerns we have. By stating that the district is making us do something gives away our power. We have a sphere of control and influence, and we need to take responsibility for our part of the work."

- **If someone says, "This time line is unrealistic":** "I don't disagree. There isn't ever enough time. I have found myself feeling the same way. I have found that looking at it this way [explain] and doing this modification in my day [explain] helped me make some time. Given that we did all agree this was an expectation, and that it isn't going away, what do you suggest that we do next?"

- **If someone says, "You know I have a point about this piece of the project! I am right," (and they are):** "You are right. This isn't okay. In previous implementations, _____ was done poorly. And I, too, am correct. [State the facts on your end.] We all have a responsibility from where we sit to be a part of the solution. I don't disagree that this hasn't moved along the way it should have. The process last time could have been a better one. And, we still need to get to the result. I will agree that [state your agreement]. Will you also agree, given that this isn't going away, we should find a way to move forward?"

- **If someone says, "You know so-and-so isn't going to do that. She's just going to check out":** "I am not discounting that _____ hasn't been an early adopter of the programs we have rolled out in the past. That is true. We can still try our best to help her see how her behavior impacts the students, what the students need, and what we need. We would like you to stay on this path yourself instead of falling sway to the negativity. Stick with it and model with your behavior as a start, and we can work on structures of accountability and systems of support to assist her too."

Deep-end leaders respond instead of react, which is why we need to be more proactive and skillful. Anticipate the concerns others might have, respond to those concerns in the most understanding light you can, and, when it gets a bit heated, reply to those concerns as professionally as possible.

Question 2: Do I Have an Awareness of How My Body Language Is Perceived so I Am Viewed as Credible or Approachable, as the Situation Requires?

This question is the most kinesthetically focused of all the questions we consider from the self-assessment. It is about your body language. How can you manage your face and your body to be congruent with your professional intent, instead of showing frustration and irritation? As previous chapters have established, leading a group of adults takes an other-focused stance, control, and agility. Responses to resistance also require deep-end leaders to be flexible and agile. This agility involves knowing when one needs to be *credible* and when one needs to be *approachable*. Michael Grinder (2007), author of *The Elusive Obvious: The Science of Non-Verbal Communication* teaches us stances that we can use to establish credibility and approachability, and both are helpful in dealing with resistance. You need to be flexible and learn to use both stances at different times to manage resistance. For example, your palms are one element of your body language that can offer a sense of credibility or approachability. According to Grinder (2007), palms up is a stance of approachability, welcoming, and hospitality, while palms down is a stance of credibility that says, "I mean business. This is serious." One stance isn't better than another. You need to know how and when to align your stance with your goal. What will be the right stance for the moment? Adjusting your body language might make you more effective in managing resistance.

Deborah Gruenfeld (Stanford Graduate School of Business, 2013), professor at the Stanford Graduate School of Business, uses the terms *authoritative* and *approachable* to refer to the same types of stances that Grinder (2007) outlines, and created a list of authoritative versus approachable behaviors that go beyond one's palms. Gruenfeld (Stanford Graduate School of Business, 2013) states people who look authoritative keep their heads still, speak in complete sentences, hold eye contact while talking, move smoothly and gracefully, occupy maximum space, lean back, slow down, spread their bodies out in a space to full comfort, and look down with their heads tilted back a bit. Both Grinder and Gruenfeld give us clues on how to manage our bodies to be more authoritative or credible. There are times when projecting strength with your body is the way to deal with resistance. Perhaps the person you are working with needs someone with a strong spine to simply say, "This is where we are headed" while maintaining strong eye contact. In these situations, the other person needs to feel your strength and assuredness and understand that you mean business. This might help with those who are used to following a leader, working in a hierarchical system with power differentials, and following the rules.

But, as noted, this isn't the only stance to take with resistance. Sometimes others want to see you as understanding and authentic. Gruenfeld (Stanford Graduate School of Business, 2013) and Grinder (2007) call this stance the *approachable stance*. People who appear approachable nod in agreement when someone is talking, smile even when what the other person is saying is not funny, start sentences with "um," speak in incomplete sentences and edit as they go, and lean in to create a more collegial atmosphere (Stanford Graduate School of Business, 2013). Approachable body language is less rigid, with more softness in the spine, and more vulnerability with one's body. This body language can help to bring others' defenses down because they see someone taking a vulnerable stance as being real, collaborative, or more compassionate. Both stances are important. It isn't an either-or. You need to know your audience and realize which stance is necessary in the moment.

You might be thinking there is a gender bias associated with these behaviors; many people find men assertive and credible when they use this body language, while they see women as too aggressive when they demonstrate the same behaviors (Cuddy, 2018). It is true that this bias exists in many contexts. The key here is to be agile, to be able to be *both* credible and approachable in your stance as the situation requires. It will take practice. I thought I needed to be far more credible when I first started consulting, and Michael Grinder (personal communication, May, 2015) told me the way to be more credible was to be more approachable because I was scaring the workshop participants with how strong I was standing! Being facile and adaptable is the key to managing yourself in the most challenging moments. When Beyoncé invokes her stage persona Sasha Fierce, she becomes bold and energetically powerful. At times, I need to do the opposite and become softer and more at ease in my body. Both credibility and approachability have their moments for a deep-end leader. Which way do you feel most comfortable being, and which way do you need to adopt more of in order to be more effective in your rollout? Visit http://leanin.org/education /power-influence for more information on ways to adopt a certain stance.

Throwing Out Resistance

Kendall Zoller and Claudette Landry (2010) speak to dealing with resistance by naming it and using hand gestures to throw it out of the room. For example, you can name the resistance by acknowledging it when speaking to a group that is resistant to an upcoming initiative: "It has been said this project is a waste of our time. It is a waste of our resources. Some might say it will take too long or it will take our time away from the other key initiative we are focused on." While making these statements, you can use body language to throw out the resistance by placing your palms facing up and gesturing toward the door in a throwing motion. You can then redirect the discussion: "And here is the information we have on why we need to focus on this" and use body language to bring attention to the information you want participants to focus on by turning toward a screen that presents the information that validates the project's importance. Finally, you can bring the focus to the group doing the work: "So together let's look at how we can address this need" (turning back to the participants, walking toward them, and using eye contact).

For more information on this practice, see Zoller and Landry (2010). Nonverbal communication can do wonders for responding effectively to resistance.

Strategies for Responding to Resistance

The following sections offer a few strategies that will help you become even more socially adept when responding to resistance.

Watch Your Language

There are differences among a suggestion, a recommendation, and an expectation. We all might think that softening up the "musts" in an implementation plan with "thoughts to consider and ideas to take a look at when you have the time" is a better way to ease into the work. It might be true *if* they are honest suggestions or ideas to consider. If you have musts, non-negotiables, mandates, or requirements, sugarcoating your language with false diplomacy will be less authentic and ultimately decrease your ability to be successful in your implementation. It isn't required that you yell or use exclamation points or be mean, but the concepts of suggestion, recommendation, and expectation are different and the wording must be accurate and consistent to have traction.

Get Rid of the Word *Can't*

Changing our mindsets and eliminating the word *can't* from our self-talk go hand in hand. In her *Forbes* article "The Amazing Power of 'I Don't' vs. 'I Can't,'" Heidi Grant Halvorson (2013) argues the power of words like *can't* when she explains:

> I don't is experienced as a choice, so it feels empowering. It's an affirmation of your determination and willpower. I can't isn't a

choice—it's a restriction, it's being imposed upon you. So thinking "I can't" undermines your sense of power and personal agency.... Because the truth is, it is your choice.

Using the word *don't* is so much more powerful and is indicative of personal agency in response to resistance.

Set Yourself Up Linguistically for Success

Mark Goulston (2013a) shares his technique for being preemptive with giving challenging feedback to a client by asking him or her:

> Going forward, in the event I have to tell you about a bump and obstacle or setback, what is the best way to tell you? . . . This is much too important for me to not get exactly right, because in the event we need to have such a conversation, I want to do it exactly as you have suggested.

This strategy sets a premise in relationships and in projects that we can anticipate bumps and obstacles, and we want to address them in a humane way. Both parties have a role to play in ensuring that interaction is done as productively as possible.

Change Your Words, Change Your Mindset

Rather than thinking a behavior is negative, reframe it to see the strength beneath it. You will be less reactive and more responsive to the individual if you see his or her behavior is coming from a place of positivity. Table 3.1 offers examples of ways to reframe the language you use to describe others' behaviors.

Table 3.1: Reframing Negative Language to Positive Language

Negative Language	Positive Language
"They are intimidating and loud."	"They are dedicated and passionate."
"They pick at every little problem."	"They are conscientious."
"They are rigid in their rule following."	"They are responsible and do what's right."
"They are obsessive in their question asking."	"They are organized."
"They don't follow any of the mandates."	"They are adaptive and flexible."

Source: Adapted from Regier, 2017.

Conclusion

All these strategies are just nuanced tips on how to change up language, one word at a time. Deep-end leaders are mindful of how they speak even when others are not. Resistance will happen. Count on it. Don't freak out. Don't lash out. Don't react. Respond.

Even with all these deep-end strategies under your belt, the challenges you face can take their toll on you mentally, physically, and psychologically. In the next chapter, we work on managing and sustaining yourself while swimming in the deep end. Swim on.

Reflection Questions

Wade into the following questions for team or individual reflection.

- Do you have a good sense of the foundational skills and norms of collaborative behavior you are working with at your school?

- Which of the linguistic responses mentioned in this chapter help you be more responsive versus reactive? Which ones seemed authentic to you, and which could you use to respond to others?

- Do you need to modify your body language to build up your credibility, approachability, or both for your initiative, depending on the nature of your communications? If so, how?

CHAPTER 4

Managing Yourself Through Change and Resistance

Breathe deeply and know that who you are can withstand the experience of conflict that living requires.

—*Mark Nepo*

In 1998, when I was diagnosed with multiple sclerosis, I learned just how real the need for managing yourself is. After a bout of optic neuritis and fatigue, my eyesight returned and my medications have kept me from relapsing. Since then, I have had two relapses when I needed infusions and had to take time off. When I said I was on my last nerve after those seventy-two-hour experiences with high-dose steroids, I was serious! But what this illness has taught me is that my health is too important to not take it seriously. I now have an extreme self-care support team. I do not consider self-care an indulgence but rather an investment. If I want to keep doing good work, this vessel I am working with has to keep going, and I have to care for it. We all need to take care of ourselves if we want to be able to have the endurance to swim in the deep end and not burn out. Sorry for the mixed metaphor, but bear with me as I move forward with some ideas to help you—whichever metaphor you choose.

The work deep-end leaders do is so complex and challenging that it can impact them mentally, physically, and psychologically. We need to build our resolve, strength, stamina, and resilience to manage the energy, change, and volatility that comes with working in schools. As joyous and worthwhile as our work is at the best of times, it is draining, exhausting, and downright debilitating at times as well.

This chapter will help you learn how to manage *yourself* through changes and roll-outs, no matter the initiative. It is about building up mental and physical resilience to handle the everyday ups and downs that come with implementing new initiatives. Learning how to stay strong amid such change is a necessity. After studying the role of resilience in this foundational deep-end skill, we'll review in detail the self-assessment questions for managing yourself through change and resistance to help you gauge your strengths and weaknesses with each item.

The Role of Resilience

Merriam-Webster's definition of *resilience* (n.d.) is "*1.* the capability of a strained body to recover its size and shape after deformation caused especially by compressive stress; *2.* an ability to recover from or adjust easily to misfortune or change." How does one recover from, adjust to, or manage to thrive in challenging circumstances? It's not a new challenge or a novel question, yet it is still a question worth asking. Our health depends on it.

Educators spend oodles of time supporting students in this work on resilience. Books like *The Gift of Failure: How the Best Parents Learn to Let Go So Their Children Can Succeed* (Lahey, 2015), *How Children Succeed: Grit, Curiosity, and the Hidden Power of Character* (Tough, 2012), *Mindset: The New Psychology of Success* (Dweck, 2006), and *Grit: The Power of Passion and Perseverance* (Duckworth, 2016) all focus on students building a sense of inner strength to take themselves through a setback or a rough patch. Many schools have mental health counselors, programs focused on social-emotional learning, and workshops to help faculty become more trauma sensitive. These items are worthy of our time and energy, and yet I have always wondered why teacher well-being wasn't at the top of the list of needs as well. On airplanes, flight attendants say, "Put on your own mask first before helping others," but in schools, we don't apply this concept of taking care of ourselves so that we're able to care for others as often as we need to.

You have to grow your physical, psychological, and emotional bandwidth to manage the complexity of deep-end work. Being able to bounce back from rejection and disappointment isn't a luxury, but a basic necessity for deep-end leaders. You need to be able to answer these three key questions in the affirmative or start on a path of self-care so you can do so in the future.

1. Am I getting better at coping with unexpected chaos and predictable high anxiety within my organization?

2. Can I soothe myself when being dismissed, diminished, challenged, or ignored?

3. In moments of discomfort, can I retain my ability to let in information and make informed, nonreactive choices and keep myself centered enough to hear different opinions in the midst of conflict?

It is always a challenge to grow up and be able to manage emotions. Self-regulation has been a mainstay of the work we do in schools for students, from keeping them from moving about on the carpet in kindergarten to not shouting out answers in discussions throughout high school. We too have our work as leaders, to manage our own emotions so we can sufficiently get beyond ourselves and stay concerned about others.

For additional information on building resilience, see appendix A (page 85), which includes a list of web resources on resilience that I recommend. Visit **go.SolutionTree .com/leadership** for a free reproducible version of this appendix.

A Deep Dive Into Self-Assessment Questions

For many of us, reading a book about self-care is not going to suffice. We need to *do* something different and create an ecosystem of resiliency support. The following sections guide your reflection on questions from your deep-end self-assessment that focus on the last of the four foundational deep-end skills—managing yourself through change and resistance—and provide a few ideas to create and implement an infrastructure in which you do not just survive change and resistance but thrive as you face these challenges.

Question 1: Do I Have Structures and Supports in Place in My Life to Help Me Physically Manage the Challenges That Will Come My Way?

You will encounter many challenges throughout your work and personal life, and part of managing them depends on physical strength and stamina. When you are physically depleted, you will feel things in a different, more highly charged way. When people are fatigued (and schools can tire you out) the last thing you want to do is exercise but research says it helps (Warner, n.d.)! Running or working out isn't an indulgence. Writer and civil rights activist Audre Lorde (1988) makes an excellent point when she says, "Caring for myself is not self-indulgence, it is self-preservation" (p. 131).

Ways to care for our bodies might include massages, movement, and healthy snack choices. According to the Mayo Clinic Staff (n.d.a), massages can alleviate headaches, alter your immune system, increase blood flow, reduce anxiety, and decrease insomnia. I ask for them as a gift when my birthday rolls around each year. And

Heidi Godman (2018), executive editor of the *Harvard Health Letter* speaks to the importance of movement and its effect on thinking skills, noting:

> In a study done at the University of British Columbia, researchers found that regular aerobic exercise, the kind that gets your heart and your sweat glands pumping, appears to boost the size of the hippocampus, the brain area involved in verbal memory and learning.

One of the heads of school I worked for had us do our midmorning and midday debriefs during walks around a nearby park. We worked in a school where if the students were only allowed healthy snacks, then so were the teachers. We ate nuts and not potato chips. Every little bit helps.

Adequate and quality sleep is another essential component we must ensure for ourselves. Lack of sleep can lead to physical and mental health problems (Huffington, 2016; National Heart, Lung, and Blood Institute, n.d.). One small step you can take to ensure better sleep involves setting limits for device use around bedtime. If you leave your phone by your bed when you go to sleep, take it off vibrate and turn off all sounds and alerts so texts and emails don't ping all night. Set up an auto-reply that says, "If this email comes in after 8 p.m. I will respond to it the next business day." Better yet, leave your phone outside your bedroom.

But you know all this. *Doing it* is another matter. Create the habits. I had a terribly sprained finger once, and while I was doing my physical therapy, my out-of-town boyfriend was visiting, and I didn't want to sleep with my splint on. I wanted to cuddle in comfort. The therapist looked straight at me and said, "Your now boyfriend or your finger. Your choice." I kept the splint on. Your current job or your life? Perspective, people.

Question 2: Do I Have a Breathing, Meditation, or Quieting Practice That Will Help Bring Calm to My Body and Mind?

I am blessed to be located near some amazing places for taking time-outs. (1440 Multiversity, Esalen Institute, Institute for Noetic Sciences, Spirit Rock, Tassajara, and Rancho La Puerta are some in the Bay Area and on the West Coast, but there are other such retreat spots or conference centers with a focus on both the intellect *and* the heart and spirit *all over* the United States and the world.) They give those who come to them time to center themselves and restore. At many of those campuses, I learned to meditate and quiet my mind. When I am not able to step out of my life for a weekend, I still start my day with a moment of silence or a guided meditation from a website like Davidji (https://davidji.com) or Insight Timer (https://insighttimer .com). I prefer guided meditations to pure silence because, as an extrovert, I engage more with the process when I am focusing on someone else's voice. The same goes for walking meditations. Giving myself something to do (either listening or moving) keeps me in the moment. There are some seven-minute sessions (I particularly like Tony Brady's [n.d.] "Re-dedication to Goodness," and the Lovingkindness meditation by Sharon Salzberg [2017] is always centering). I also use them for calming before I go to bed. These moments of quiet lower my heart rate and my blood pressure, and reminding myself to be in the moment and calming my body are always good things.

Question 3: Do I Take Time to Cultivate Relationships in My Life Outside Work?

A 2017 *Harvard Business Review* article by former Surgeon General Vivek H. Murthy cites an AARP report (Wilson & Moulton, 2010) that states 40 percent of the adults in America report feeling lonely. Murthy (2017) writes, "Loneliness was often in the background of clinical illness, contributing to disease and making it harder for patients to cope and heal." This idea of connecting to others isn't neediness; it is human. We need a life-work balance. The love we receive and give in our lives *outside* of work helps us stay healthy, and maintaining a work-life supports this while also providing benefits such as improved and increased productivity and increased feelings of control in one's work life (Anderson, Coffey, & Byerly, 2002; Arthur, 2017; Casper & Harris, 2008; Robinson, 2015). It cannot be discounted. I maintain these relationships by intentionally seeking out my friends on a regular basis, making plans to go out for meals, and I make a special effort to visit with friends when I am in their hometowns and they are in mine. It matters. A snuggle with my six- and eight-year-old nephews and their two dogs isn't bad either.

Question 4: Do I Have a Structure in My Life for Acknowledging the Good That Is Going on or a Method of Expressing Gratitude on a Continual Basis?

Oprah Winfrey (OWN, 2012; 2017) and so many others talk about their gratitude practices. There are gratitude journals on Amazon and articles galore on websites touting the importance of gratitude. There is research stating that if we focus on the positive it will make us happier, diminish depression, and immeasurably improve our lives (Emmons, 2008).

Danny Bauer (personal communication, 2017), the host of the podcast *Better Leaders Better Schools* (https://betterleadersbetterschools.com), shared with me that he has a journaling practice every morning that includes writing down three things he is grateful for, one thing he is excited about for that day, and one person he is going to try to help without need for reciprocity. I don't have a practice of daily journaling, but I sure do say the Jewish prayer the Shehecheyanu an awful lot. While it is intended for special occasions and celebrations to thank God for bringing us to this wonderful moment, I use it after many a workshop or a coaching experience where I acknowledge my gratitude for being a part of an amazing experience. Everything is a celebration. Further, expressing gratitude improves romantic and family relationships and makes us more effective in our work as well (Ackerman, 2017; Algoe, Fredrickson, & Gable, 2013). I toast "L'chaim!" ("To life!") as often as I can, and I even thank my apartment when I leave for a trip for holding a space for me to come back to.

Question 5: Am I Aware of the Concept of a Growth Versus Fixed Mindset, and How Am I Working With It in My Own Life and Work?

While previous chapters in this book focus on the need to understand others' development of a continuous growth mindset, have you considered your own? In what areas do you see yourself with a fixed mindset you would like to shift? I often think about my self-talk and my fixed mindset mentality around certain things I think I can and cannot do. Oh, the limiting beliefs we hold! Carol Dweck (2006) speaks to the stretch language of working on something and not achieving it *yet*. *Yet* reframes the way we think about items we may want to improve on. For example, instead of saying, "I am not a very good cook" after burning a meal, we can say, "I am not a very good cook *yet*" to give ourselves the opportunity to regard the failure as a learning experience and to plan to try again and learn from our mistakes.

The same applies in our work as deep-end leaders. I also work on reminding myself struggle is good, that growing and progress—not just the product or outcome—are important to me and that I can substantially change, stretch, and grow, *and* it is fun. I know this mindset shift takes time, but believing in these concepts and looking at mistakes through a different lens helps me work with a growth mindset on a daily basis.

For a fun tool to get you in a pumped-up mood about the idea of adding *yet* to your vocabulary and self-talk, visit https://bit.ly/1tYtrmT to check out Janelle Monae performing the song "Power of Yet" on *Sesame Street*.

Question 6: Do I Have Self-Talk That Is Optimistic, and Am I Learning to Be More Optimistic? (Do I Have a Coach or Someone Who Works With Me on My Self-Talk and Helps Me Look at My Assumptions, Belief Systems, and Strengths?)

This question, again, focuses on those limiting beliefs and self-talk that hold you back. It might not be something that we all do, but I sure do have an adversary in my head that talks to me and tells me I cannot do certain things—that certain tasks or behaviors aren't appropriate or right or easy enough for me—and thus I don't move ahead. I have a name for my adversary. Do you? In a workshop I attended, we named and addressed our adversaries. We asked them a few questions.

- "What is your name?"
- "Why do you prevent the changes (fill in with your name) wants to make?"
- "What do you need from (fill in your name)?"
- "What do you want from (fill in your name)?"
- "When were you born?"
- "Is there anything (fill in your name) can do to let you go?"

It was incredibly helpful to name my limiting belief adversary and *separate her from me*. The more I say, "Oh, that's _____ talking" the easier it is for *me* to move ahead and feel that a challenge is doable.

And given that I am a coach, and I have had a coach, I strongly endorse the use of external support to assist with this work. If you can find someone who works for your district and understands the district context and the dynamics, and who is helpful for your deep-end implementation, great. Having people in this role from outside the district can be a good idea as well. They will not have past experiences with the district that will lead them to approach the work in a counterproductive way, and they can focus on you and your process, not their histories and understandings of the dynamics.

I am also a huge fan of reframing situations using learned optimism. Martin Seligman (2012) wrote *Learned Optimism* as a pessimist who was working on seeing things from another perspective. *Learned optimism* is a way of looking at setbacks in our lives through a more "glass half full" lens and retraining our thought patterns to be more positive. In the deep end, we need to see things in a more optimistic way because we are going to come up against roadblocks and need to reframe the bumps as positively as possible. See www.authentichappiness.sas.upenn.edu for more on Seligman's work.

When I worked in the classroom, I would give the following talk when I handed out the first paper of the semester: "If you don't feel you did as well as you had hoped, you need to say three things to yourself: (1) this is *just one paper* (think short term— not permanence), (2) it doesn't mean anything about you as a person, or as a student in the bigger sense (it is not a global or pervasive reflection of you), and (3) you can work on it again (more effort and change of behavior will help—it's not personal)."

I have thought through those three Ps (*permanence, pervasiveness,* and *personalization*) on many a ride to an airport as I left a less-than-stellar workshop I facilitated, or after I received a "we went with someone else" email in which I didn't get the job. As Alain de Botton (2013) states, "One of the greatest gifts is that of being good at disappointment: having nonpersecutory, speedy, resilient emotional digestion." Thinking about these sorts of disappointments lacking permanence and pervasiveness or remembering that they are not personal can help move you from getting depressed to getting over them more quickly.

Question 7: Do I Have a Compassion Practice That Includes Both Self-Compassion and Loving Kindness for Others?

The Greater Good Science Center at UC Berkeley (https://greatergood.berkeley .edu) and the Center for Compassion and Altruism Research and Education at Stanford University (http://ccare.stanford.edu) both do wonderful work on *loving kindness meditations* and *self-compassion meditations* (see Kristin Neff's work at www .self-compassion.org as well). Loving kindness meditations are meditations in which one takes time to cultivate compassion for him- or herself and others. A person sits in contemplation and with a tender heart thinks about oneself and others he or she knows (family and friends) and doesn't know (strangers and the world) with care and compassion. I also do self-compassion meditations with a focus on loving oneself unconditionally. It isn't always easy for me, as I have found myself being a bit ill-tempered, having said something snarky, or not having managed my impulsivity and raised my voice, and I feel bad about it. Once I have cleaned up what I messed up, and apologized to the person, I try to move on and do better next time. I try not to beat myself up. Deep-end leaders must have more self-compassion in moments when we falter, or we won't be able to get done what needs to get done. If we keep living in the past, we can't move forward to doing things better in the future. Self-compassion meditations help me honor my humanity and acknowledge I am human and mess up, and that is okay, but also urge me to reflect on what I can I do better next time.

I also encourage you to check out Fred Luskin's work (2001) at the Stanford Forgiveness Project if you need to be more forgiving of others. Forgiveness is not only good for our relationships with others but is also good for our immune systems! An article published on The Johns Hopkins Hospital (Johns Hopkins Medicine, n.d.) website explains:

> Chronic anger puts you into a fight-or-flight mode, which results in numerous changes in heart rate, blood pressure and immune response. Those changes, then, increase the risk of depression, heart disease and diabetes, among other conditions. Forgiveness, however, calms stress levels, leading to improved health.

Forgiveness is not just for them but also for you.

Question 8: Do I Take Time Out for inspirational Moments That Bring Me Back to Why I Do What I Do for Students and Ground Me in the Importance of Doing Deep-End Work?

I am not advocating for any specific way of seeking out inspiration, but we are certainly in need of some hope and inspiration as deep-end leaders. University of Rochester psychologists Todd M. Thrash and Andrew J. Elliot (2003) note, "The heights of human motivation spring from the beauty and goodness that precede us and awaken us to better possibilities" (p. 887). We have more creativity when we have experienced an inspirational moment, a better chance of progress in moving forward with one's goals, and an increase in well-being. Take that hike in nature, watch that TED Talk, attend a worship service, or watch a preschool graduation or a middle school orchestra concert. Go to the theater. Go to a movie and be amazed at the special effects. See a sports team doing its level best to win. Watch the Olympics. Feel something. Do it often. Put it in your calendar as a must-do, just like flossing and taking your vitamins. It matters.

Question 9: Do I Have Plans to Grow Myself and My Skill Sets?

For so many reasons that include the lack of funds, resources, and time, I sadly watch administrators and leaders get the *least* amount of professional development in a school. While teachers do need to learn the newest classroom curriculum or the most recent research-based ways to engage English learners, only some leaders from a school site are intentional and fortunate enough to join their teachers in the study of that new content. Many leaders are back at their desks completing other work because there is too much management to be done and not enough learning time for us all. And yet, the necessary learning around leadership is deep and broad and requires as much time and support as any other role in the system. It's important to support all educators' growth just as much as we support students' growth.

Understandably, time is a factor. Before- and after-school session times fill up with district meetings or individualized education programs. Summer is also necessary for vacation and rest. We need to be discerning about choices for professional learning, but absolutely keep it on the front burner. Following are five ways I have identified for leaders to ensure they keep learning.

1. **Join a mentoring group such as a mastermind group:** In addition to hosting the *Better Teachers Better Schools* podcast as mentioned in the section on question 4, Danny Bauer is a former principal who is now, among other roles, a mastermind group facilitator. Mastermind groups are peer-to-peer mentoring organizations that support group members in developing leadership skills. His group is global and provides an excellent support system of like learners who thrive on growth and hold each other accountable to do great things back at their sites. Visit https://betterleadersbetterschools.com/mm to learn more about this mastermind group, or search for mastermind groups for educators online and see if there are groups in your area.

2. **Attend a conference with intention:** Choose wisely. I am always delighted with my time at the preconferences at Learning Forward's annual conferences (www.learningforward.org). Preconferences take place over the weekend ahead of the conference and provide the opportunity to attend full-day sessions with excellent presenters you might not ever get a chance to see in your school district or within your region, who not only know their content but how to facilitate adult learning.

3. **Join a terrific professional development group or network:** My go-to is one that Learning Omnivores (http://learningomnivores.com) created. This group of district leaders, teachers, and consultants are so busy facilitating adult learning opportunities that they realized we needed our own group to meet with and learn from. The group members, of which I am one, determine who they would like to learn from (for example, thought leaders such as Yong Zhao, Carol Dweck, and Margaret Wheatley) and arrange to meet with that person at his or her location. We reserve our own rooms at a hotel, arrange for a meeting room, and book our flights. We meet as a group to learn from an expert and then talk among ourselves about how the content

applies to our own contexts. You can make up your own Learning Omnivores group and do one locally. Share the wealth.

4. **Take online courses, listen to podcasts, and engage in Twitter chats:** For those of us who have other commitments that require us to work on our learning asynchronously or prevent us from attending conferences for days at a time or going on weekend retreats, there are other terrific ways to learn. Short-term options include Twitter chats, which could take thirty to sixty minutes, or podcasts, which could be thirty to forty-five minutes in a car or on a walk. Slightly longer options might be a summit of videos that could take a week to get through, or a course that would take eight weeks of more committed work with assignments. You do it on your own time, during your commute or after you put the kids to bed. Finding a community is the key; you follow up on ideas as you wish.

   Following are some blogs I read and cool podcasts I have had the pleasure to listen to or be interviewed for.

   • *Beyond the Staff Room* with Derek Rhodenizer (https://voiced .ca/beyond-the-staffroom)

   • *The Personal Playlist Podcast* with Noa Daniel (https://voiced .ca/the-personal-playlist-podcast-with-noa-daniel)

   • Jon Harper's *My Bad Podcast* (https://jonharper.blog/my -bad-podcast)

   • *Principal Center Radio* (www.principalcenter.com/radio)

5. **Keep reading lists:** I am always asking others what they are reading. I have a friend, Bill Sommers, a former principal in different states and districts and currently a consultant and coach, who is the most voracious reader I know. He travels hundreds of thousands of miles on planes, during which he reads (and reads and reads) mostly nonfiction leadership books and creates book summaries for all the books. He has hundreds of unpublished summaries he shares with colleagues. He is remarkable. If you, too, are a voracious reader and are interested in his book notes, send me an email at jennifer@jenniferabrams.com, and I will connect you. You can also reach out to colleagues and friends for suggestions. It's good to have friends and colleagues like Bill who can curate a reading list for you, once you are done reading all sources in this book's bibliography, of course.

Question 10: Do I Take Time for Restorative Moments?

I was quite serious when I wrote in *The Multigenerational Workplace: Communicate, Collaborate & Create Community* (Abrams, 2016) that when baby boomers were younger, they never took sick days unless they had a compound fracture and pneumonia, and if it was just one of those, they still showed up! I think it is true that dedication to work was paramount for that generation. Nowadays mental health preservation and self-care are also important, and people are really reterming a *work-life balance* as a *life-work balance*. This phenomenon is real; NPR did a piece in 2017 titled "The Millennial Obsession With Self-Care" (Silva, 2017), and *Forbes* published an article titled "Practicing Self-Care Is Important: 10 Easy Habits to Get You Started" (Nazish, 2017). Self-care is touted and it's mocked, but I believe in it. Some may wonder whether this has to do with younger teachers being more indulged, or if people are starting to pay more attention to the research that says we need to give ourselves more time-outs to restore ourselves.

In a *Harvard Business Review* article, authors Justin Talbot-Zorn and Leigh Marz (2017) write:

> Recent studies are showing that taking time for silence restores the nervous system, helps sustain energy, and conditions our minds to be more adaptive and responsive to the complex environments in which so many of us now live, work, and lead.

And this need for silent time is doubly true if you are an introvert. Michael Godsey's (2016) post "Why Introverted Teachers Are Burning Out" in *The Atlantic* says:

> In some ways, today's teachers are simply struggling with what the Harvard Business Review recently termed "collaborative overload" in the workplace. According to its own data, "over the past two decades, the time spent by managers and employees in collaborative activities has ballooned by 50% or more." The difference for teachers in many cases is that they don't get any down time; they finish various meetings with various adults and go straight to the classroom, where they feel increasing pressure to facilitate social learning activities and promote the current trend of collaborative education. This type of schedule and expectation for constant social interaction negates the possibility to psychologically "recharge" in relative solitude, something that's crucial to many introverts.

So take that *me day* so you don't have to retire early.

In fact, I would take some time off *every* time there is a holiday or a break. I try to get out of the country if I can because, for me, it's the best way to truly get away. But it's not essential to go far; staycations can be incredibly beneficial. You can also design your own stay-at-home retreat. See Cherry (2017), Easterly (n.d.), and Louden (1997) for ideas for staycations if going too far from home isn't in the cards.

Question 11: Do I Notice That I Laugh Every Day? Do I Put Myself in Situations That Make Me Smile?

Life is a gift. You *can* smile. It might not be your default expression, but it is good for you. Laughter and smiling change your physiology (Heid, 2014; Savage, Lujan, Thipparthi, & DiCarlo, 2017). Laughing enhances your ability to take in oxygen, activates your stress response, and calms you down (Heid, 2014; Mayo Clinic Staff, n.d.b). Laughing can improve your immune system, relieve pain, and lessen your depression (Rosenfeld, 2018). When genuine, smiling can indicate greater general wellbeing, marital satisfaction, and possible longevity (Jaffe, 2010). And according to Ron Gutman (TED, 2011), "British researchers found that one smile can generate the same level of brain stimulation as up to 2,000 bars of chocolate."

We can increase our smiling and laughing simply by exposing ourselves to things we find amusing. Read *New Yorker* cartoons. Go for Netflix's comedians section on a particularly ho-hum evening. See TheDodo.com for silly animal videos. Do whatever it takes. It's the cheapest therapy around.

Question 12: Do I Have Moments When I Can Experience Giving in a Different Way Outside My Work, Perform Acts of Service, or Attend Events That Support Causes?

Many educators might say we give more at the office than most; we aren't paid as well as other professions; we pay out of our pocket for school supplies. We go to school board meetings and chaperone and advise and support. It is true. However, outside of school, we can also vote, sign petitions, attend community events, and volunteer. Contributor for the Cleveland Clinic's *Health Essentials* blog Scott Bea (2016) calls the feeling you get from volunteering and working in some form for the social good a *helper's high*. Bea (2016) explains, "According to a study published in the *International Journal of Psychophysiology*, people who gave social support to others had lower blood pressure than people who didn't. Supportive interaction with others also helped people recover from coronary-related events." And—this should make us educators all feel better—he goes on to include that, when compared with those who do not volunteer, people fifty-five and older volunteering for at least two organizations were 44 percent less likely to die within five years (Bea, 2016).

There is so much to give, and now, with more life to live, more time in which to do it.

Conclusion

The ideas in this chapter are just that, ideas. Please don't think you must consider all these questions on a daily basis. Any of these actions or readings would then just seem like an addition to your to-do list, and that isn't the intention. We all just need to keep swimming, so do what it takes to keep yourself going. Take a moment, drink a protein shake, get a coach, do Aikido. Whatever you choose, just keep moving, and don't give up on yourself. You are the only you you've got.

Reflection Questions

Wade into the following questions for team or individual reflection.

- Which of the self-care strategies mentioned in this chapter are you already doing?

- Which of the self-care strategies seem appealing? Will you look into incorporating them more frequently into your life?

- What two things can you do in the next twenty-four hours to make sure you add more self-care to your day-to-day work?

What's Next?

Each of you is perfect the way you are . . . and you can use a little improvement.

—Shunryu Suzuki (Suzuki Roshi)

These four leadership skills—(1) thinking before you speak, (2) preempting resistance, (3) responding to resistance, and (4) managing yourself through change and resistance—will serve you well on your leadership journey, but in the spirit of Suzuki Roshi, the Shunryu Suzuki Zen monk and teacher who helped popularize Zen Buddhism in the United States (Chadwick, 2001), we are just getting started and we all can "use a little improvement." I know there is much more we could dive into here just in this book—more about project management and large-group facilitation, more about adult development and conflict resolution, and more about how to manage overwhelming circumstances and build resilience. I encourage you to find an item that presents a learning edge and go for it with more study and a deeper dive. We are just getting started. It's a wonderful journey.

Resources for Diving Deeper

Use the following four resources and those listed in appendices A and B (pages 85–89) to continue your deep-end work on an item that presents a personal learning edge for you. Visit **go.SolutionTree.com/leadership** for free reproducible versions of these appendices.

1. Ontario Leadership Framework (https://bit.ly/2wWhjbY; Institute for Education Leadership, 2013) suggests two additional approaches for building your skills.

a. Systems thinking

- Having the ability to comprehend the complexity of a large organization and the various moving parts that work interdependently within it, along with having the foresight to anticipate likely upcoming challenges

b. Proactivity

- Having the ability to plan ahead and effectively anticipate and then manage change on a large scale and in challenging moments

- Showing initiative and grit as one moves an organization ahead in a meaningful way.

2. The future-thinking educational organization KnowledgeWorks (2015; https://bit.ly/2E6fYWB) offers a forecast that looks ahead to the next decade. They encourage readers to "explore the opportunities and challenges raised by this ten-year forecast and to consider what role you might play in shaping the future of learning." If that isn't the deep end, I am unsure what is.

3. Jennifer Garvey Berger and her work at the organizations Cultivating Leadership (www.cultivatingleadership.co.nz) and Growth Edge Coaching (www.growthedgecoaching.com) really push us to work in the deep end and learn how to manage complexity with more sturdiness. These two organizations offer blogs, certification information, and both in-person and online workshops and coaching that support leaders' growth in their deep-end work rather than retreating to the shallow end.

4. Laura van Dernoot Lipsky's (http://traumastewardship.com) and Margaret J. Wheatley's (https://margaretwheatley.com) work help leaders working to develop trauma sensitivity and strength to support those in chaotic times. Books, articles, podcasts, workshops and additional resources are available these for those who are interested in this work.

In the end, everyone has swim in their own lane and determine what the deep end looks like for them. It might be that after answering the questions in the introduction (see figure I.2, pages 9–11) you find that swimming in the deep end in a school system and leading change isn't the right thing to do at this time on your journey, and that is okay. There are other ways to contribute and effect change. You might find yourself wanting to contribute to the education of others from another vantage point and take on a different role. Know yourself. Place yourself in an environment where your talents and abilities shine. Don't stay where you will be unhealthy and unhappy. There is so much for us to do, so if you want to change your role, that's okay, too. Just keep swimming. We need you in the water.

Final Reflection Questions

Wade into the following questions for team or individual reflection.

- What's still alive for you as you end this book?

- What crossroads are you at as you finish this book?

- What has been most worthy of your time as you read this book?

- What has your attention at this point?

- What matters to you now?

- What did you learn from this book that will allow you to interrupt the ways things are done in terms of rolling out initiatives at your site?

- What deep-end conversations can you have that will bring something new into the world?

- What was of meaning or value to you as a result of reading this book?

- What flame do you want to carry into all interactions from here on that will cement some deep-end work you are doing?

- What declaration do you want to make in terms of your commitment to swim in the deep end?

- What strikes you as important to share, discuss, or reflect on at this time?

- What is your next deep-end learning goal?

APPENDIX A

Websites That Inspire and Support Resilience

The following bloggers have been instrumental in developing my resilience, helping me be an adult, and supporting me to become a better human being. I encourage you to use these resources for support in your own deep-end journey. Visit **go.SolutionTree.com/leadership** for a free reproducible version of this appendix.

- **Superhero Life (www.superherolife.com):** Creator Andrea Scher explains, "I'm redefining what it means to be a SUPERHERO—'cause in my world, it's got nothing to do with capes, spandex or sidekicks and everything to do with tenderness, intuition & baby steps of bravery."

- **Mark Manson (www.markmanson.net):** The author of *The Subtle Art of Not Giving a F*ck*, Manson hopes to "give life advice that doesn't suck."

- **Seth Godin (http://sethgodin.typepad.com):** Inspirational blogger and author Seth Godin "focuses on everything from effective marketing and leadership, to the spread of ideas."

- **On Being (www.onbeing.org):** Terrific journalist and interviewer Krista Tippett leads the On Being Project, "an independent non-profit public life and media initiative that pursues deep thinking and social courage, moral imagination and joy."

- **Brain Pickings (www.brainpickings.org):** Maria Popova writes a terrific and "free Sunday digest of the week's most interesting and inspiring articles across art, science, philosophy, creativity, children's books, and other strands of our search for truth, beauty, and meaning."

- **Eric Barker (Barking Up the Wrong Tree—www.bakadesuyo.com /blog):** Eric Barker, author of *Barking Up the Wrong Tree* writes a blog which, he notes, "brings you science-based answers and expert insight on how to be awesome at life."

- **Gaping Void (www.gapingvoid.com):** Gaping Void is a culture design group that focuses on human design and change, and offers a blog with terrific visuals that inspire.

- **Next Avenue (www.nextavenue.org):** "Where grown-ups keep growing" is the tag line for this website that offers "vital ideas, context and perspectives on issues that matter most as we age."

- **The School of Life (www.theschooloflife.com):** This global London-based organization offers emotional intelligence development workshops worldwide and has a fabulous shop and a great blog.

- **Center for Courage and Renewal (www.couragerenewal.org):** This site aims to connect people and empower diverse communities. The center offers workshops that help participants rejoin "soul and role," a terrific set of resources, and a blog.

- **Margaret J. Wheatley (www.margaretwheatley.com):** I am a big fan of Margaret Wheatley, author extraordinaire. She features articles, videos, and books on her site that align with her work on helping us become warriors for the human spirit.

- **Bobbi Emel (www.thebounceblog.com):** Emel is a therapist who writes a blog for people who want to bounce back from challenging events. Resources on developing resilience, bouncing back from grief, and knowing your core gifts are found on the site.

APPENDIX B
Additional Recommended Websites

The following websites align with the four foundational skills in this book. Please look to them for additional resources around these key skills. Visit **go.SolutionTree .com/leadership** for a reproducible version of this appendix.

All Four Foundational Skills

- **Ontario Ministry of Education Leadership Development: Framework (www.edu.gov.on.ca/eng/policyfunding/leadership /framework.html):** The inspiration for this book came from working with educational leaders at the Ontario Ministry of Education Leadership Development and using the framework they offer on this site.

Thinking Before You Speak

- **Farnam Street (https://fs.blog):** Farnam Street focuses on helping readers understand the world and live a better life, focusing on topics such as mental models, decision making, learning, reading, and the art of living. This website offers links to blogs, articles, podcasts, books, and so on, all on how to think more productively.

Preempting Resistance

- **The Choices Project at Brown University (www.choices.edu):** Based at Brown University, The Choices Project is a nonprofit organization that develops curricula on current and historical international and public policy issues and offers professional development for educators. In each curricular unit, a central activity challenges students to consider multiple viewpoints on a contested issue. The work asks students to be allocentric in focus and could be a starting point for creating curricula for adults to do the same.

- **Civil Politics (www.civilpolitics.org):** Civil Politics is a nonprofit organization run by a group of academics whose expertise lies in the use of data to understand moral psychology. The website features research on civility and offers educational resources, links, and videos for those who are interested in communication across divides.

- **Geert Hofstede (www.geerthofstede.com):** Geert Hofstede is a Dutch social psychologist who did a pioneering study of cultures across modern nations. His biography and research are featured on his website.

- **Global Fluency Institute (www.globalfluency.org):** Using a foundation of internationally acclaimed research and resources, the Global Fluency Institute aims to support lifelong global fluency development by providing "individuals with the KNOWLEDGE, tools, skills, and mindset to function successfully in an interconnected, culturally diverse world."

- **National Equity Project (www.nationalequityproject.org):** National Equity Project's mission is to "dramatically improve educational experiences, outcomes, and life options for students and families who have been historically underserved by their schools and districts." It provides workshops on social emotional learning and equity and its website provides publications, resources, and tools.

- **Turner Consulting Group (www.turnerconsultinggroup.ca):** Turner Consulting Group, focused on creating a diverse workforce and inclusive work environment offers free infographics such as the Diversity Wheel and self-assessments on inclusive classrooms, which are helpful for leaders when in their work around preempting resistance.

- **YourMorals (www.yourmorals.org):** This website run by social psychology professors and students at the University of Virginia, The University of California (Irvine), and the University of Southern California allows readers to explore their morality, ethics, and values. It has been helpful for me and those I work with to take the quizzes on the site and discuss how we look at given issues through a lens of what is moral and how others might see things differently.

Responding to Resistance

- **National School Reform Faculty (www.nsrfharmony.org):** NSRF provides resources and training that promotes effective collaboration among educators around the world. The workshops train facilitators to use specific protocols that allow all participants' voices to be heard and honored as they give nonjudgmental, but open and honest feedback to one another. The skills around collaboration participants learn in these workshops help them build their linguistic ability to give feedback in humane and growth-producing ways.

Managing Yourself Through Change and Resistance

- **The Center for Compassion and Altruism Research and Education at Stanford University (CCARE; ccare.stanford.edu):** The center does research, workshops, and conferences focusing on compassion and altruism. Videos and blogs can be found on its website.

- **Greater Good Science Center (http://greatergood.berkeley.edu):** The University of California, Berkeley has a center that reports on groundbreaking research into the roots of compassion, happiness, and altruism. It hosts a summer conference for educators, provides workshops, and offers lectures year-round that focus on wellbeing.

- **Hervé da Costa (www.herve.com):** Hervé is an executive coach who focuses on leadership and inter and intrapersonal intelligence. He is a great blend of cognitive and spiritual brainpower.

- **Self-Compassion (www.self-compassion.org):** Kristen Neff is a leader in the work of self-compassion and did pioneering research in the field.

- **Sharon Salzberg (www.sharonsalzberg.com):** Salzberg is known for her work in meditation and is an author, workshop leader, and major figure in the work around loving kindness.

References and Resources

Abrams, J. (2009). *Having hard conversations*. Thousand Oaks, CA: Corwin Press.

Abrams, J. (2016). *Hard conversations unpacked*. Thousand Oaks, CA: Corwin Press.

Abrams, J., & von Frank, V. (2014). *The multigenerational workplace: Communicate, collaborate and create community*. Thousand Oaks, CA: Corwin Press.

Ackerman, C. (2017, April 12). *The benefits of gratitude: 28 questions answered thanks to gratitude research*. Accessed at http://positivepsychologyprogram.com/benefits -gratitude-research-questions on September 7, 2018.

Aguilar, E. (2013). *The art of coaching: Effective strategies for school transformation*. San Francisco: Jossey-Bass.

Aguilar, E. (2016). *The art of coaching teams: Building resilient communities that transform schools*. San Francisco: Jossey-Bass.

Algoe, S. B., Fredrickson, B. L., & Gable, S. L. (2013). The social functions of the emotion of gratitude via expression. *Emotion, 13*, 605–609.

Amabile, T., & Kramer, S. (2011, March). The power of small wins. *Harvard Business Review*. Accessed at https://hbr.org/2011/05/the-power-of-small-wins on January 2, 2019.

Anderson, S. E., Coffey, B. S., & Byerly, R. T. (2002). Formal organizational initiatives and informal workplace practices: Links to work-family conflict and job-related outcomes. *Journal of Management, 28*(6), 787–810.

Arbinger Institute. (2010). *Leadership and self-deception: Getting out of the box*. Oakland, CA: Berrett-Koehler.

Aronson, E. (2015). *Mistakes were made (but not by me): Why we justify foolish beliefs, bad decisions and hurtful acts*. Boston: Mariner.

Arrien, A. (2007). *The second half of life: Opening the eight gates to wisdom*. Louisville, CO: Sounds True.

Arthur, M. M. (2017). Share price reactions to work-family initiatives: An institutional perspective. *Academy of Management Journal, 46*(4), 497–505.

Baddeley, A. (1994). The magical number seven: Still magic after all these years? *Psychological Review, 101*(2), 353–356.

Barker, E. (2017a). 5 questions that will make you emotionally strong [Blog post]. *Barking Up the Wrong Tree.* Accessed at www.bakadesuyo.com/2017/03/emotionally-strong on September 7, 2018.

Barker, E. (2017b). *Barking up the wrong tree: The surprising science behind why everything you know about success is (mostly) wrong.* New York: HarperCollins.

Bea, S. (2016, November 15). *Wanna give?: This is your brain on a "helper's high."* Accessed at https://health.clevelandclinic.org/why-giving-is-good-for-your-health on September 7, 2018.

Bennett, J. (2015, August 1). I'm not mad: That's just my RBF. *The New York Times.* Accessed at www.nytimes.com/2015/08/02/fashion/im-not-mad-thats-just-my-resting-b-face.html on September 7, 2018.

Benson, J. (2012). 100 repetitions. *Educational Leadership, 70*(2), 76–78.

Benson, J. (2014). *Hanging in: Strategies for teaching the students who challenge us most.* Alexandria, VA: Association for Supervision and Curriculum Development.

Berger, J. G. (2012). *Changing on the job: Developing leaders for a complex world.* Palo Alto, CA: Stanford University Press.

Berger, J. G., & Johnston, K. (2016). *Simple habits for complex times.* Palo Alto, CA: Stanford Business Books.

Block, P. (2003). *The answer to how is yes: Acting on what matters.* Oakland, CA: Berrett-Koehler.

Block, P. (2009). *Community: The structure of belonging.* Oakland, CA: Berrett-Koehler.

Block, P. (2013). *Stewardship: Choosing service over self-interest* (2nd ed.). Oakland, CA: Berrett-Koehler.

Brady, T. (n.d.). *Begin again: Re-dedication to goodness.* Accessed at https://insighttimer.com/tonybrady/guided-meditations/begin-again-re-dedication-to-goodness on September 7, 2018.

Brown, B. (2017). *Braving the wilderness: The quest for true belonging and the courage to stand alone.* New York: Random House.

Carter, J. R., & Palihawadana, M., (Eds.). (2000). *The Dhammapada: The sayings of the Buddha*. New York: Oxford University Press.

Casper, W. J., & Harris, C. M. (2008). Work-life benefits and organizational attachment: Self-interest utility and signaling theory models. *Journal of Vocational Behavior, 72*(1), 95–109.

Chadwick, D., (Ed.). (2001). *Zen is right here: Teaching stories and anecdotes from Shunryu Suzuki, author of* Zen Mind, Beginner's Mind. Boston, MA: Shambhala Publications.

Cherry, R., (2017). *How to plan a staycation wellness retreat at home.* Accessed at www.shape.com/lifestyle/fit-getaways/how-plan-staycation-wellness-retreat-home on January 3, 2019.

Cialdini, R. (2016). *Pre-suasion: A revolutionary way to influence and persuade.* New York: Simon & Schuster.

Costa, A., & Garmston, R. (2015). *Cognitive coaching: Developing self-directed leaders and learners.* Norwood, MA: Christopher-Gordon.

Covey, S. M. R. (2008). *The speed of trust: The one thing that changes everything.* New York: Simon & Schuster.

Cuddy, A., (2018). *Presence: Bringing your boldest self to your biggest challenges.* Boston: Back Bay Books.

de Botton, A. [alaindebotton]. (2013, December 3). One of the greatest gifts is that of being good at disappointment: having non persecutory, speedy, resilient emotional digestion [Tweet]. Accessed at https://twitter.com/alaindebotton/status/408847113205075968 on January 3, 2019.

Delistraty, C. C. (2014). The psychological comforts of storytelling. *The Atlantic.* Accessed at www.theatlantic.com/health/archive/2014/11/the-psychological-comforts-of-storytelling/381964 on January 2, 2019.

DeWitt, P. M. (2017). *Collaborative leadership: Six influences that matter most.* Thousand Oaks, CA: Corwin Press.

Donohoo, J. (2017). *Collective efficacy: How educators' beliefs impact student learning.* Thousand Oaks, CA: Corwin Press.

Drago-Severson, E., & Blum-DeStefano, J. (2016). *Tell me so I can hear you: A developmental approach to feedback for educators.* Cambridge, MA: Harvard Education Press.

Dressler, L. (2012). *Standing in the fire: Leading high-heat meetings with clarity, calm, and courage*. Oakland, CA: Berrett-Koehler.

Duckworth, A. (2016). *Grit: The power of passion and perseverance*. New York: Scribner.

Dweck, C. (2006). *Mindset: The new psychology of success*. New York: Ballantine.

Easterly, E. (n.d.). *12 ways to create a stay-at-home yoga retreat*. Accessed at https://chopra.com/articles/12-ways-to-create-a-stay-at-home-yoga-retreat on January 3, 2019.

Ebbinghaus, H. (1913). *Memory: A contribution to experimental psychology*. (H. A. Ruger & C. E. Bussenius, Trans.). New York: Teachers College, Columbia University.

Emmons, R. (2008). *Thanks!: How practicing gratitude can make you happier*. Boston: Mariner Books.

Frank, C., & Magnone, P. (2011). *Drinking from the fire hose: Making smarter decisions without drowning in information*. London: Penguin.

Freedman, M. (2013). How do you manage upward?: The coauthor of *Influencing Up* describes how to build a partnership with the boss. *Stanford Business*. Accessed at www.stanfordbusiness-online.com/stanfordbusiness/autumn-2013?pg=32#pg32 on September 6, 2018.

Fullan, M., & Quinn, J. (2015). *Coherence: The right drivers in action for schools, districts and systems*. Thousand Oaks, CA: Corwin Press.

Garmston, R. (2018). *The astonishing power of storytelling: Leading, teaching, and transforming in a new way*. Thousand Oaks, CA: Corwin Press.

Garmston, R., & Wellman, B. (1999). *The adaptive school: A sourcebook for developing collaborative groups*. Norwood, MA: Christopher-Gordon.

Garmston, R., & Zimmerman, D. (2013). *Lemons to lemonade: Resolving problems in meetings, workshops and PLCs*. Thousand Oaks, CA: Corwin Press.

Godin, S. (2014). *What to do when it's your turn (and it's always your turn)*. Hastings-on-Hudson, NY: The Domino Project.

Godman, H. (2018). *Regular exercise changes the brain to improve memory, thinking skills*. Accessed at www.health.harvard.edu/blog/regular-exercise-changes-brain-improve-memory-thinking-skills-201404097110 on December 21, 2018.

Godsey, M. (2016, January 25). Why introverted teachers are burning out. *The Atlantic*. Accessed at www.theatlantic.com/education/archive/2016/01/why-introverted-teachers-are-burning-out/425151 on September 7, 2018.

GOOD Magazine. (2016). *If the world were 100 people* [Video file]. Accessed at www
.youtube.com/watch?v=QFrqTFRy-LU on January 3, 2019.

Goulston, M. (2013a, April 2). How to deal with a toxic client [Blog post]. *Harvard
Business Review*. Accessed at https://hbr.org/2013/04/how-to-deal-with-a-toxic
-clien on September 7, 2018.

Goulston, M. (2013b, November 15). Don't get defensive: Communication tips
for the vigilant [Blog post]. *Harvard Business Review*. Accessed at http://blogs
.hbr.org/2013/11/dont-get-defensive-communication-tips-for-the-vigilant on
September 6, 2018.

Goulston, M. (2016). *Talking to crazy: How to deal with irrational and impossible
people in your life*. New York: American Management Association.

Grant, A. (2014a, October 1). *Emotional intelligence is overrated*. Accessed at www
.psychologytoday.com/blog/give-and-take/201410/emotional-intelligence-is
-overrated on September 6, 2018.

Grant, A. (2014b). *Give and take: Why helping others drives our success*. New York:
Penguin.

Grinder, M. (2007). *The elusive obvious: The science of non-verbal communication*.
Battle Ground, WA: Michael Grinder & Associates.

Haidt, J. (2012). *The righteous mind: Why good people are divided by politics and
religion*. New York: Pantheon.

Halvorson, H. G. (2013). *The amazing power of "I don't" vs. "I can't."* Accessed at
www.forbes.com/sites/heidigranthalvorson/2013/03/14/the-amazing-power-of-i
-dont-vs-i-cant on September 6, 2018.

Hammond, Z. (2015). *Culturally responsive teaching and the brain: Promoting
authentic engagement and rigor among culturally and linguistically diverse students*.
Thousand Oaks, CA: Corwin Press.

Hargreaves, A., & O'Connor, M. T. (2018). *Collaborative professionalism: When
teaching together means learning for all*. Thousand Oaks, CA: Corwin Press.

Heath, C., & Heath, D. (2010). *Switch: How to change things when change is hard*.
New York: Crown Business.

Heath C., & Heath, D. (2013). *Decisive: How to make better choices in life and work*.
New York: Crown Business.

Heid, M. (2014). You asked: Does laughing have real health benefits? *TIME*. Accessed
at http://time.com/3592134/laughing-health-benefits on February 5, 2019.

Heschel, A. J. (1953). The spirit of Jewish education. *Jewish Education*, *24*(2), 9–20.

Hicks, D. (2011). *Dignity: Its essential role in resolving conflict.* New Haven, CT: Yale University Press.

Hirschmann, A. (1991). *The rhetoric of reaction: Perversity, futility, jeopardy.* Boston: Belknap Press.

Hollis, J. (2006). *Finding meaning in the second half of life: How to finally, really grow up.* New York: Avery.

Hofstede, G. & Hofstede, G. J., & Minkov, M. (2010). *Cultures and organizations: Software of the Mind—Intercultural cooperation and its importance for survival* (3rd ed.). New York: McGraw-Hill.

Huffington, A. (2016). *The sleep revolution: Transforming your life, one night at a time.* New York: Harmony.

Impedovo, M. A., & Malik, S. K. (2016). Becoming a reflective in-service teacher: Role of research attitude. *Australian Journal of Teacher Education*, *41*(1). Accessed at https://ro.ecu.edu.au/cgi/viewcontent.cgi?referer=https://www.google.com/&httpsredir=1&article=2877&context=ajte on January 2, 2019.

Institute for Education Leadership. (2013, September). *The Ontario leadership framework: A school and system leader's guide to putting Ontario's leadership framework into action.* Paris, ON, Canada: Author.

Jaffe, E. (2011). The psychological study of smiling. *Association for Psychological Science.* Accessed at www.psychologicalscience.org/observer/the-psychological-study-of-smiling on January 2, 2019.

Johns Hopkins Medicine. (n.d.). *Forgiveness: Your health depends on it.* Accessed at www.hopkinsmedicine.org/health/healthy_aging/healthy_connections/forgiveness-your-health-depends-on-it on January 3, 2019.

Joseph, D. L., & Newman, D. A. (2010). Emotional intelligence: An integrative meta-analysis and cascading model. *Journal of Applied Psychology*, *95*(1), 54–78. Accessed at http://dx.doi.org/10.1037/a0017286 on September 6, 2018.

Kang, S. H. K. (2016). Spaced repetition promotes efficient and effective learning: Policy implications for instruction. *Policy Insights From the Behavioral and Brain Sciences*, *3*(1), 12–19. Thousand Oaks, CA: SAGE.

Kaufman, S. B. (2011, November 8). Why inspiration matters. *Harvard Business Review.* Accessed at https://hbr.org/2011/11/why-inspiration-matters on September 7, 2018.

Keen, S. (2010). *In the absence of God: Dwelling in the presence of the sacred.* New York: Harmony.

Keen, S. (2016). *What's next? Reviewing and revisioning our lives.* Esalen Institute workshop, Big Sur, CA.

Kegan, R., & Laskow Lahey, L. (2001). *How the way we talk can change the way we work: Seven languages for transformation.* San Francisco: Jossey-Bass.

Kegan, R., & Laskow Lahey, L. (2009). *Immunity to change: How to overcome it and unlock the potential in yourself and your organization.* Boston: Harvard Business Review Press.

Kegan, R., & Laskow Lahey, L. (2016). *An everyone culture: Becoming a deliberately developmental organization.* Boston: Harvard Business Review Press.

Killion, J. (2015). *The feedback process: Transforming feedback for professional learning.* Oxford, OH: Learning Forward.

Kise, J. A. G. (2014). *Unleashing the positive power of differences: Polarity thinking in our schools.* Thousand Oaks, CA: Corwin Press.

KnowledgeWorks. (2015). *KnowledgeWorks Forecast 4.0: The future of learning—Education in the era of partners in code.* Accessed at https://knowledgeworks.org/wp-content/uploads/2018/01/forecast-4.pdf on October 8, 2018.

Lahey, J. (2015). *The gift of failure: How the best parents learn to let go so their children can succeed.* New York: HarperCollins.

Lakoff, G., & Johnson, M. (2003). *Metaphors we live by.* Chicago: University of Chicago Press.

Laloux, F., & Wilber, K. (2014). *Reinventing organizations.* Millis, MA: Nelson Parker.

Lambert, L., Walker, D., Zimmerman, D. P., Cooper, J. E., Lambert, M. D., Gardner, M .E., & Szabo, M. (2002). *The constructivist leader* (2nd ed.). New York: Teachers College Press.

Lambert, L., & Zimmerman, D. (2016). *Liberating leadership capacity: Pathways to educational wisdom.* New York: Teachers College Press.

LaPorte, D. (2014). *The desire map: A guide to creating goals with soul.* Louisville, CO: Sounds True.

Lee, B. (1997). *The power principle: Influence with honor.* New York: Fireside.

Lerner, H. (2001). *The dance of connection: How to talk to someone when you're mad, hurt, scared, frustrated, insulted, betrayed or desperate.* New York: HarperCollins.

Lerner, H. (2004). *The dance of fear: Rising above anxiety, fear, and shame to be your best and bravest self.* New York: HarperCollins.

Lerner, H. (2017). *Why won't you apologize?: Healing big betrayals and everyday hurts.* New York: Touchstone Press.

Lieberman, M. D. (2013). *Social: Why our brains are wired to connect.* New York: Crown.

Lipton, L., & Wellman, B. (2013). *Learning-focused supervision: Developing professional expertise in standards-driven systems.* Burlington, VT: Miravia.

Lorde, A. (1988) *Burst of light and other essays.* Ithaca, NY: Firebrand Books.

Lorde, A. (2007). *Sister outsider: Essays and speeches.* Berkeley, CA: Crossing Press Feminist Series.

Louden, J. (1997). *The woman's retreat book.* San Francisco, CA: Harper Collins.

Luskin, F. (2001, August). *Effects of group forgiveness intervention on perceived stress, state and trait, anger, symptoms of stress, self-reported health and forgiveness (Stanford Forgiveness Project).* Accessed at https://learningtoforgive.com/research/effects -of-group-forgiveness-intervention-on-perceived-stress-state-and-trait-anger -symptoms-of-stress-self-reported-health-and-forgiveness-stanford-forgiveness -project on September 7, 2018.

Lyubomirsky, S., Sheldon, K., & Schkade, D. (2005). Pursuing happiness: The architecture of sustainable change. *Review of General Psychology, 9*(2), 111–131.

Markus, H. R., & Conner, A. (2013). *CLASH: 8 cultural conflicts that make us who we are.* New York: Hudson Street Press.

Marshak, R. J. (2006). *Covert processes at work: Managing the five hidden dimensions of organizational change.* Oakland, CA: Berrett-Koehler.

Mayo Clinic Staff. (n.d.a). *Massage: Get in touch with its many benefits.* Accessed at www.mayoclinic.org/healthy-lifestyle/stress-management/in-depth/massage/art -20045743 on December 21, 2018.

Mayo Clinic Staff. (n.d.b). *Stress relief from laughter? It's no joke.* Accessed at www .mayoclinic.org/healthy-lifestyle/stress-management/in-depth/stress-relief/art -20044456 on February 5, 2019.

McDonald, J. P., Mohr, J., Dichter, A., & McDonald, E. C. (2003). *The power of protocols: An educator's guide to better practice.* New York: Teachers College Press.

McLaren, K. (2010). *The language of emotions: What your feelings are trying to tell you.* Louisville, CO: Sounds True.

Meyer, E. (2014). *The culture map: Breaking through the invisible boundaries of global business*. New York: Public Affairs.

Molinsky, A. (2013). *Global dexterity: How to adapt your behavior across cultures without losing yourself in the process*. Boston: Harvard Business Review Press.

Monae, J. (2014, September 10). *Sesame Street: Janelle Monae—Power of yet* [Video file]. Accessed at www.youtube.com/watch?v=XLeUvZvuvAs on September 7, 2018.

Muhammad, A. (2009). *Transforming school culture: How to overcome staff division*. Bloomington, IN: Solution Tree Press.

Murthy, V. (2017). Work and the loneliness epidemic. *Harvard Business Review*. Accessed at https://hbr.org/cover-story/2017/09/work-and-the-loneliness -epidemic on September 7, 2018.

National Heart, Lung, and Blood Institute. (n.d.). *Sleep deprivation and deficiency*. Accessed at www.nhlbi.nih.gov/health-topics/sleep-deprivation-and-deficiency on January 3, 2019.

Nazish, N. (2017). *Practicing self-care is important: 10 easy habits to get you started*. Accessed at www.forbes.com/sites/payout/2017/09/19/practicing-self-care-is -important-10-easy-habits-to-get-you-started/#34bd5039283a on January 2, 2019.

Neff, K. (2012). *Self-compassion: The proven power of being kind to yourself*. New York: William Morrow.

Nepo, M. (2000). *The book of awakening: Having the life you want by being present to the life you have*. San Francisco: Conari Press.

Newport, C. (2016). *Deep work: Rules for focused success in a distracted world*. New York: Grand Central.

O'Hara, M., & Leicester, G. (2012). *Dancing at the edge: Competence, culture and organization in the 21st century*. Devon, United Kingdom: International Futures Forum.

OWN. (2012). *Oprah's Gratitude Journal*. Accessed at www.oprah.com/oprahs -lifeclass/oprah-on-the-importance-of-her-gratitude-journal-video on January 2, 2019.

OWN. (2017). *Oprah readers entries from her first gratitude journal | The Oprah Winfrey Show | OWN* [Video file]. Accessed at www.youtube.com /watch?v=VyMrZ5RbL54 on January 2, 2019.

Palmer, P. J. (1998). *The courage to teach: Exploring the inner landscape of a teacher's life*. San Francisco: Jossey-Bass.

Platt, A. D., Tripp, C. E., Ogden, W. R., & Fraser, R. G. (2000). *The skillful leader: Confronting mediocre teaching*. Concord, MA: Ready About Press.

Porter, J. (2017, March 21). Why you should make time for self-reflection (even if you hate doing it). *Harvard Business Review*. Accessed at https://hbr.org/2017/03/why-you-should-make-time-for-self-reflection-even-if-you-hate-doing-it on September 6, 2018.

Porter, S. (2009). *Relating to adolescents: Educators in a teenage world*. Lanham, MD: Rowman & Littlefield.

Principal Life. (n.d.). Accessed at www.facebook.com/groups/PrincipalLife on November 9, 2018.

Regier, N. (2017). *Conflict without casualties: A field guide for leading with compassionate accountability*. Oakland, CA: Berrett-Koehler.

Resilience. (n.d.). In *Merriam-Webster's online dictionary*. Accessed at www.merriam-webster.com/dictionary/resilience on September 7, 2018.

Reynolds, G. (2011). *Presentation Zen: Simple ideas on presentation design and delivery* (2nd ed.). New York: New Riders.

Rilke, R. M. (1993). *Letters to a young poet* (M. D. Herter, Trans.). New York: Norton.

Robinson, J. (2015). *The science of work-life balance*. Accessed at www.worktolive.info/work-life-balance-research on January 3, 2019.

Rock, D. (2008). SCARF: A brain-based model for collaborating with and influencing others. *NeuroLeadership Journal, 1*.

Rock, D. (2009). *Your brain at work: Strategies for overcoming distraction, regaining focus, and working smarter all day long*. New York: Harper Business.

Rosenfeld, J. (2018). *11 scientific benefits of having a laugh*. Accessed at http://mentalfloss.com/article/539632/scientific-benefits-having-laugh on February 5, 2019.

Salzberg, S. (2014). *Real happiness at work: Meditations for accomplishment, achievement, and peace*. New York: Workman Press.

Salzberg, S. (2017, August 14). *Guided Lovingkindness meditation from Sharon Salzberg*. Accessed at https://soundcloud.com/mindfulmagazine/guided-mettalovingkindnessmeditation-from-sharon-salzberg on September 7, 2018.

Sandberg, S. (2013). *Lean in: Women, work, and the will to lead.* New York: Knopf.

Sasse, B. (2017). *The vanishing American adult: Our coming-of-age crisis and how to rebuild a culture of self-reliance.* New York: St. Martin's Press.

Savage, B. M., Lujan, H. L., Thipparthi, R. R., & DiCarlo, S. E. (2017). Humor, laughter, learning, and health! A brief review. *Advances in Physiology Education, 41*(3), 341–347. Accessed at www.ncbi.nlm.nih.gov/pubmed/28679569 on February 5, 2019.

Schein, E. H. (2013). *Humble inquiry: The gentle art of asking instead of telling.* Oakland, CA: Berrett-Koehler.

Scott, S. (2004). *Fierce conversations: Achieving success at work and in life one conversation at a time.* New York: Berkley Publishing Group.

Seligman, M. (2012). *Learned optimism: How to change your mind and your life.* New York: Vintage.

Sheridan, R. (2015). *Joy, Inc.: How we built a workplace people love.* New York: Penguin.

Shipman, C., & Kay, K. (2014). *The confidence code: The science and art of self-assurance—What women should know.* New York: Harper Business.

Silva, C. (2017). *The millennial obsession with self-care.* Accessed at www.npr.org /2017/06/04/531051473/the-millennial-obsession-with-self-care on January 2, 2019.

Slap, S. (2010). *Bury my heart at conference room B: The unbeatable impact of truly committed managers.* New York: Penguin.

Slap, S. (2015). *Under the hood: Fire up and fine-tune your employee culture.* New York: Penguin.

Stanford Graduate School of Business. (2013). Debra Gruenfeld: *Power & Influence* [Video file]. Accessed at www.youtube.com/watch?v=KdQHAeAnHmw on January 2, 2019.

Steele, D. M., & Cohn-Vargas, B. (2013). *Identity safe classrooms: Places to belong and learn.* Thousand Oaks, CA: Corwin Press.

Stone, D., & Heen, S. (2014). *Thanks for the feedback: The science and art of receiving feedback well.* New York: Viking.

Talbot-Zorn, J., & Marz, L. (2017, March 17). The busier you are, the more you need quiet time. *Harvard Business Review.* Accessed at https://hbr.org/2017/03 /the-busier-you-are-the-more-you-need-quiet-time on September 7, 2018.

Tannen, D. (1995). The power of talk: Who gets heard and why. *Harvard Business Review*. Accessed at https://hbr.org/1995/09/the-power-of-talk-who-gets-heard-and-why on January 2, 2019.

Tamm, J. W., & Luyet, R. J. (2005). *Radical collaboration: Five essential skills to overcome defensiveness and build successful relationships.* New York: Harper Business.

TED. (2011). *Ron Gutman: The hidden power of smiling* [Video file]. Accessed at www.ted.com/talks/ron_gutman_the_hidden_power_of_smiling?language=en#t-331639 on January 3, 2019.

Thrash, T. M., & Elliot, A. J. (2003). Inspiration as a psychological construct. *Journal of Personality and Social Psychology, 84*(3), 871–889.

Tierney, J. (2011, August 17). Do you suffer from decision fatigue? *New York Times.* Accessed at www.nytimes.com/2011/08/21/magazine/do-you-suffer-from-decision-fatigue.html on September 6, 2018.

Tippett, K. (2017). *Becoming wise: An inquiry into the mystery and art of living.* New York: Penguin.

Tough, P. (2012). *How children succeed: Grit, curiosity, and the hidden power of character.* New York: Houghton Mifflin Harcourt.

Tracy, B. (2010). *How the best leaders lead: Proven secrets to getting the most out of yourself and others.* New York: American Management Association.

Tufte, E. (1990). *Envisioning information.* Cheshire, CT: Graphics Press, LLC.

U.S. Department of State. (n.d.). *Passport statistics.* Accessed at https://travel.state.gov/content/travel/en/passports/after/passport-statistics.html on September 7, 2018.

Visually. (n.d.). *Infographic design.* Accessed at https://visual.ly/product/infographic-design on January 3. 2019.

Waldschmidt, D. (2014). *Edgy conversations: How ordinary people can achieve outrageous success.* Austin, TX: Next Century.

Warner, J. (n.d.). *Exercise fights fatigue, boosts energy.* Accessed at www.webmd.com/diet/news/20061103/exercise-fights-fatigue-boosts-energy on January 3, 2018.

Wedell-Wedellsborg, T. (2013). *Innovation as usual: How to help your people bring great ideas to life.* Boston: Harvard Business Review Press.

Wedell-Wedellsborg, T. (2017, January–February) Are you solving the right problems? *Harvard Business Review.* Accessed at https://hbr.org/2017/01/are-you-solving-the-right-problems on January 2, 2019.

Wellman, B., & Lipton, L. (2004). *Data-driven dialogue: A facilitator's guide to collaborative inquiry*. Charlotte, VT: MiraVia.

Wheatley, M. J. (2006). *Leadership and the new science: Discovering order in a chaotic world* (3rd ed.). San Francisco: Berrett-Koehler.

Wheatley, M. J. (2010). *Perseverance*. Oakland, CA: Berrett-Koehler.

Wheatley, M. J. (2012). *So far from home: Lost and found in our brave new world*. Oakland, CA: Berrett-Koehler.

Wheatley, M. J. (2017). *Who do we choose to be?: Facing reality, claiming leadership, restoring sanity*. Oakland, CA: Berrett-Koehler.

Wilson, C., & Moulton, B. (2010). *Loneliness among older adults: A national survey of adults 45+*. Washington, DC: AARP. Accessed at https://assets.aarp.org/rgcenter/general/loneliness_2010.pdf on January 3, 2019.

Wiseman, L., Allen, L., & Foster, E. (2013). *The multiplier effect: Tapping the genius inside our schools*. Thousand Oaks, CA: Corwin Press.

Zoller, K., & Landry, C. (2010). *The choreography of presenting: The 7 essential attributes of effective presenters*. Thousand Oaks, CA: Corwin Press.

Index

Stronger Together
Terri L. Martin and Cameron L. Rains
How do I build collaborative teams that support a common vision? How do I tap into others' skills? New and veteran leaders ask themselves these questions. *Stronger Together* will help you face your current reality and determine steps for improvement.
BKF792

Step In, Step Up
Jane A. G. Kise and Barbara K. Watterston
Step In, Step Up guides current and aspiring women leaders in education through a twelve-week development journey. An assortment of activities, reflection prompts, and stories empower readers to overcome gender barriers and engage in opportunities to learn, grow, and lead within their school communities.
BKF827

Messaging Matters
William D. Parker
Harness the power of messaging to create a culture of acknowledgment, respect, and celebration. Written specially for leaders, this title is divided into three parts, helping readers maximize their role as chief communicators with students, teachers, parents, and community.
BKF785

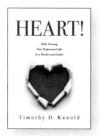

HEART!
Timothy D. Kanold
Explore the concept of a heartprint—the distinctive impression an educator's heart leaves on students and colleagues during his or her professional career. Use this resource to reflect on your professional journey and discover how to foster productive, heart-centered classrooms and schools.
BKF749

Solution Tree | Press
a division of
Solution Tree

Visit SolutionTree.com or call 800.733.6786 to order.

Wait! Your professional development journey doesn't have to end with the last pages of this book.

We realize improving student learning doesn't happen overnight. And your school or district shouldn't be left to puzzle out all the details of this process alone.

No matter where you are on the journey, we're committed to helping you get to the next stage.

Take advantage of everything from **custom workshops** to **keynote presentations** and **interactive web and video conferencing**. We can even help you develop an action plan tailored to fit your specific needs.

Let's get the conversation started.

Call 888.763.9045 today.